Live Your Ultimate Life

Ancient Wisdom to Harness Success, Health and Happiness

Live Your Ultimate Life

Ancient Wisdom to Harness Success, Health and Happiness

Dr. Mao Shing Ni
Author of Secrets of Longevity

TAO OF
WELLNESS
PRESS

Published by
Tao of Wellness Press
An Imprint of SevenStar Communications 1412 14th Street, Santa Monica,
CA 90404
www. taoofwellness.com

Cover and icon design by Justina Krakowski
Book design by Dana Martin

Contents

Introduction...9

Part 1: You..**15**

1 The Wood Element..21
2 The Fire Element...41
3 The Earth Element...59
4 The Metal Element...77
5 The Water Element...95

Part 2: Your Life..**113**

6   Physical Health..117
7   Mind Health...155
8   Relationship Health..183
9   Financial Health...209
10 Career Health..233

Part 3: Your Dreams & Wishes.................................**253**

11 Map Out Your Destination.....................................259
12 The Journey of Your Life and
     Infinichi Coaching..281

Conclusion: Share Your Successes,
     Leave Your Legacy..305

Appendix...323
Index...347
Resources..351

Introduction

Everyone wants to be happy. But few ever achieve that universally desired state of joy and bliss, because most people are looking for that one "Holy Grail"—promising to make them "live happily ever after!" Happiness eludes many of us because we've bought into the myth that it is a thing you achieve, rather than a state of being.

True happiness comes from a life well lived, and is the byproduct of finding health, balance and fulfillment in the physical, emotional, spiritual, social and financial aspects of your life.

On the journey to a happy life, you must start with the fundamental understanding of who you are, why you are here and where you want to go. You need to know these things because self-discovery is the basis to achieving your life. It is only through self-discovery that your life becomes purposefully driven, and that you can answer the calling of your spirit and trust the path that your life desires to take.

Without knowing your strengths and weaknesses and your deep spiritual nature, you cannot recognize the behavioral patterns that you replay day in and day out and that lead to satisfaction or disappointments. By learning about these self-created "blockages" in your life, you can work on constructive changes that help you understand yourself and achieve your full potential.

Your Life
Purpose

There are seven billion human lives on planet Earth, so why are you here? None of us among the seven billion are exactly the same, not even identical twins. You have come with a unique gift, and that gift is YOU, which defines the fundamental purpose of your life. In the process of finding your full potential, you will naturally manifest this purpose by being, living and doing.

Your purpose is the compass that sets the direction of your life's journey. There are countless ways to express yourself and to manifest your life. Carefully consider where you want to go, because while the possibilities are endless you don't want to be constantly changing direction. If you should find yourself on the wrong path, however, don't be afraid to change it.

Applying Ancient Wisdom
for a Successful Future

We humans are complex beings, composites of Nature and Nurture. Nature includes genetics from your ancestors, intelligence, personality traits and your unique talents. Nurture includes the way you were raised by your family, experiences in schools, and your interactions with others and your environment. And underlining all this is the subtle but powerful cosmic influence that shapes your unique personality.

Humans have evolved over millions of years and are subject to the universal laws that gave birth to us and govern the entire universe. Eight thousand years ago, in China, these universal laws were written down in secret code in a book called the I Ching or the Book of Changes.

The I Ching provided a blueprint of the laws of the universe and the predictable changing patterns of nature. Historically, the insights from the I Ching aided farmers in ensuring a prosperous harvest and helped people to stay healthy and to heal from disease. Chinese emperors used the I Ching to govern their country and its people. Remarkably, the I Ching also gave rise to modern mathematical and scientific advancements, including astronomy, the binary language for computing and the keys to the genetic code.

Of utmost importance to me, and what I highlight in this book, is how the I Ching describes the secret to living a long, happy and healthy life. That secret lies in the discovery of the Five Element Personality Type, a profound guide to achieving health and fulfillment. Five Elements is the name given by the I Ching to the relationship between the cycles of life on Earth, the seasons of the year, the interaction between bodily organ systems and the properties of medicinal herbs...to mention just a few.

The I Ching refers to the five elements as Wood, Fire, Earth, Metal and Water. Not surprisingly, wise people in all parts of the world have come to the same descriptions of naturally-occurring phenomenon. Ancient Asian cultures, classic Greeks and Medieval Europeans all used very similar systems when describing the cycles of nature.

The I Ching revealed that each person is a composite of all five elements but with a core, dominant element that best defined his or her personality traits. By knowing your core Element, you can learn what your tendencies are and leverage your strength to achieve personal greatness, overcome weaknesses and release blockages that prevent you from actualizing your full potential. In other words, you will learn and apply the strategic wisdom and practices designed by the ancient masters, and in the process strengthen your physical health, restore peace within your mind, improve your relationships, increase your wealth, and experience passion and meaning in your chosen work.

Three Parts to Your Health
and Happiness

This book is organized into three parts. Part One will help you discover what your Element/Personality Type is—in other words, who you are. This is where you will learn to recognize your positive and negative personality tendencies.

Part Two will show you how your element/personality type impacts the major areas of your life, be it career, relationships and finance as well as your mind and body.

Part Three will guide and coach you, step by step, to implement strategies and solutions for transforming your negative traits while accentuating your positive attributes as you cultivate health, balance and happiness in your life and actualize your dreams.

This book shows you how you can, wherever you are, achieve success, happiness, wellbeing and fulfillment. I invite you to start your personal journey of health and happiness today!

Dr. Mao Shing Ni

Part One

You

Who are you?

Since times immemorial, humans have been asking the same, recurring question, "Who am I?" The gift of consciousness gave rise to awareness of the Self and the ability to discern similarities and differences. There is no question that you are unique; there is not another person on our planet of 7 billion exactly like you. Yet it is also true that there are patterns of personality, behavior, and health tendencies that are predictable amongst all people.

We are a product of the universe. The laws that govern nature also govern you and me. These natural laws of the universe, which the Chinese called Tao, shape everything in our world, and have evolved a predictable pattern of phenomena and changes.

Many ancient cultures have recorded these phenomena through sophisticated calendar systems, including the ancient Chinese, Egyptian, and Mayan civilizations.

In China, this predictive system was written down in one of the oldest books in the world—The I Ching or the Book of Changes. Central to the I Ching are The Five Elements, a way of understanding the interconnectedness of the world, and the process of change and transformation. The I Ching elegantly and precisely captured cyclical changes in the universe, and elucidated that human beings are the small universe, or the microcosm, of the larger universe. The wisdom of the I Ching became the fundamental guiding principle for the development of such diverse fields as Chinese medicine, binary language for computers, and human genetics.

The application of these analytical systems helped forecast weather patterns, which was essential for the successful development of agrarian societies, and laid the foundation for our modern world. After all, it was the development of agriculture that was responsible for people settling in larger and larger groups, from their earlier, hunter-gatherer ancestors. In the I Ching, the predictive modeling of The Five Elements was the forerunner of today's data-driven forecasting sciences, which are applied in meteorology, sociology, economics, and many other fields. The Five Elements are: Wood, Fire, Earth, Metal and Water. In nature there are many material and energetic expressions and representations of each Element. Similarly, in humans, there are the Five Element Personality Types, each embodying the unique characteristics of that Element.

Each of the Elements is also described with an adjective due to their corresponding personality expressions. Wood Element is called the Authoritative Type. Fire Element the Passionate Type. Earth Element is the Caring Type. Metal Element is the Methodical Type and

Water Element is the Wise Type. Just as seasonal and planetary cycles are predictable, so are human behavior and personality patterns. The Five Elements Personality categorization has been studied, recorded and utilized for thousands of years in China to help doctors advise patients on preventive health and healing. Employers hire the right person for a job, and matchmakers pair compatible couples in marriage. The secret knowledge of The Five Elements is even more relevant for our complex, ever-changing modern world.

The wisdom of The Five Elements reveals not only personality disposition, but also physical and behavioral tendencies that impact all areas of life. These include health, relationships, career and finances. Everyone possesses all Five Elements, but there is one core or dominant Element in you that expresses your Personality Type. Each Element possesses unique strengths and weaknesses, personality, temperament, and health tendencies. By understanding your core Element and using tools from this book, you will be able to remove obstacles from your path, and leverage your strength to achieve your full potential.

It is important to note that one Element isn't better or worse than others, but rather, that we are all a composite of all the Five Elements. It's just that one Element stands out more than the others. For instance, you may discover yourself to be the Metal Element/

Methodical Type. Your ultimate goal is to have balanced personality, so that you display the best attributes of all the Five Elements. Just like the seasons, and the cyclical changes—each brings a positive virtue that comprises wholeness of life.

So what Element are you? How about your boss? Your potential love interest? Your child? How do you overcome your Elemental weaknesses? How can you balance all five Elements? You will discover the answers to these questions, and learn so much about yourself and others in your life, by studying the Elements, revealed in the I Ching.

Read Chapters 1-5 to learn about your Element or log on to www.infinichi.com and take the online Five Element Quiz to receive immediate results.

Chapter 1
The Wood Element
Authoritative Personality

In the east where sun rises there is a gentle wind that awakens all. It is a movement that promotes green woody growth. When the wind is gentle it harmonizes and fertilizes like in spring, but when it is extreme as in a windstorm it can be destructive, just as in people, emotion turns into rage when the Wood Element is out of control.

The Yellow Emperor's Classic of Medicine

You Are Authoritative,
Confident and Intense

As a Wood Element/Authoritative person, you tend to be highly motivated and have a very strong personality that some identify as Type A. You are authoritative, confident, intense, smart, decisive and responsible. Wood personality is usually characterized as positive and charismatic—you command respect and make a good manager.

To Begin, to Change
and to Initiate

The Wood Element begins its phase on the first day of spring. It evokes "spring fever," the expansive moment of inception, birth and coming alive after the cold, quiet and contemplative days of winter. Wood is the renewal; the beginning of a circular cycle in which day follows night, night follows day, spring follows winter, and on and on. Just as this period in nature provokes the awakening of change, so it is in you to initiate creativity and an exciting path towards success.

Break on Through
to the Other Side

Wood energy is active, growing and expanding. It is a strong and potent force, capable of breaking through the hard shell of a seed, and pushing its way up through the soil to bask in the sunlight. The tiny seed grows up to become a tall, strong tree, bridging heaven and earth, which bears fruit to benefit us all. Nothing shall stand in your way as you break on through to the other side.

Seize the Day
Carpe Diem

Wood Element is associated with vision and foresight, coupled with the momentum to move forward. When your Wood energy flows freely, you are creative, focused, and courageous. You can achieve greatness by having clarity of vision and thoughtful planning, then unleashing your Wood Elemental energies to seize the day—Carpe Diem!

Your Liver
and Gallbladder Network

Wood Element corresponds with the liver and gallbladder network in the human body. The liver operates like nature's factory, receiving and repackaging nutrients for growth while safely removing decaying toxins at the same time. Therefore, Wood Element persons are most vulnerable in their livers. In Chinese medicine, the liver network also encompasses the ability to freely express one's emotions. When feelings are suppressed or blocked, this impacts imbalances in the liver network leading to physical symptoms like hopelessness, abdominal bloating, indigestion and resentment.

Highly Tuned
and Tightly Wound

When your Wood Element is off balance, you
can appear to be stubborn or inflexible and seem
overbearing, competitive or controlling to others. You
may want to "break through" in order to get your own
way. Your highly tuned, tightly wound nervous system
provides focus and drive, but you can also be overly
sensitive, emotional, and get easily thrown off when
you don't channel this energy in a way that keeps others
motivated as well. Knowing yourself is the first step to
restoring balance within your Wood Element.

Cultivate Strength
From Flexibility

Your challenge is to readjust after running into an obstacle, rather than trying to bulldoze through it and becoming angry or frustrated when you don't get what you want. A healthy Wood personality is like a determined ant...if one direction is blocked, the ant scurries about until it finds another way around an obstacle. A healthy Wood person is flexible yet strong. You listen and learn from others, arrive at a balanced point of view, then push forward with extraordinary creativity and remarkable, forward-moving energy.

Balanced Element,
Balanced Personality

Wood energy is manifested as growth. When it is in balance, Wood energy is naturally authoritative and articulate, and leads by positive persuasion. When it is out of balance, a Wood person can become an aggressive go-getter. Untamed Wood energy can easily lead to regretful missteps, such as saying things you don't mean in the heat of an argument or storming out of a meeting. It's important to balance your Wood Element in order to find success, happiness, harmony and contentment.

Watch Out
for Stress

If your Elemental Wood energy is in balance, you are a charismatic leader, someone who gathers people around you and makes exciting things happen. However you may be impatient for things and people to change, and if that change doesn't happen according to your timetable you can become frustrated. Remember that stress comes along with change. If your Wood Element is unbalanced, the stress will cause your liver energy to become blocked, or toxic. A careless diet, endless stress, recreational drugs and alcohol weaken liver energy and create a brittle nervous system.

Learn to Deal
With Resistance

If you are out of balance, you can be angry, accusatory, cross or aggressive which in turn causes resistance on the part of others. When you feel threatened by resistance, you may become manipulative or forceful in order to try to get your own way. Instead, listen and try to address the other person's needs first before pushing your agenda. You will achieve your goals far more easily by listening and acknowledging others.

Don't Get Stuck
in Your Liver

Interestingly, as an authoritative personality, you can be so picky and particular about making choices that you become the opposite—indecisive and stuck. In that case, you may find yourself lacking a clear and compelling direction and unable to move ahead. This block in your liver network can cause you to feel sad, depressed, resentful or unacknowledged. Go for a walk, get moving and practice tai chi to unblock your liver energy.

Impulsivity
is Your Achilles

Wood persons need to pay attention to impulsivity because quick decisions may not serve them well. If your intuition is colored by rebellion, resentment or anger, you can create problems for yourself and those around you. Calm your intensity first, gather more data, give it more thought and then ask yourself, "Do I need to make this decision now?" If it's not time-sensitive, wait 24 hours or a few days and then come back to it. You will be more clear-headed and likely to make the right choice.

Green
is Your Color

Green is the primary color of the Wood Element. It's
the color of the forest, a blade of grass and spring on a
snow-covered mountainside. The chlorophyll in green
leafy vegetables, which expresses the green color, is
a beneficial support for liver's detoxification function.
Green is good for the eyes and strengthens vision, which
is the bodily sense associated with the Wood Element.
Incorporate green to support healthy Wood energy.

Watch Out for Your Tendons
and Ligaments

The Wood Element is also represented in the human body by tendons and ligaments, the rubber band-like tissue that connects muscles to the bones and joints and enables motion. Wood imbalance may make you feel stiff and limit your range of motion and mobility. You are used to moving quickly with agility and speed so anything that slows you down causes frustration. Vulnerability to injuries and muscle strain and discomfort only further aggravates your impatience. Practice chi gong, tai chi or yoga and stretch regularly to increase your flexibility and avoid injuries.

Morning
is Your Hour

As a Wood person, your time of day is the morning, when the world is new and fresh. Open the blinds or curtains in the morning to allow the light to awaken you. An appreciation of nature comes naturally to you, so an early-morning walk in the fresh air can help you burn off your extra energy and quiet yourself. Use this personal time to relax and discover new ideas flowing into your creative mind. You can use this practice to see people and situations in a new light.

Your Soul Expresses
Through Your Dreams

Spiritually, the Wood Element relates to the soul. Your soul beckons to you in your dreams at night when you are asleep. The soul processes your daytime encounters and sensory experiences and puts you in touch with your unconscious and the spirit world. If your Wood Element is out of balance, you will have disturbed dreams; dreams of fighting, aggression, fleeing and disharmony. If there is inner turmoil or feelings that are trapped, you will wake up with a warning dream. Be quiet, pay attention and listen to your soul, which is the voice of intuition.

Cultivate
Your True Nature

You must strengthen your root; you cannot grow and thrust upward without deepening your understanding of spirituality and of life. Take a moment and reassess your goals...why do you want to go there? Is it because you want to gratify your ego? When you are able to differentiate between the artificial ego and your true nature, you will get clarity and be able to plot your course, step by step. By practicing your chi gong or tai chi, you are refining your Wood energy, strengthening your spirit and nourishing your soul.

The Wood Element
Herbal Formula

The herbal formulation in Wood Element promotes an authoritative, positive, focused and flexible spirit by supporting a healthy liver network, which further nurtures detoxification and nervous system function. The Wood Element formula is infused with chrysanthemum flower that is traditionally used to calm the intensity of authoritative Wood, dandelion herb to aid the cleansing functions and cassia seeds to empower clarity of vision so that you can confidently choose the right path for your life.

Chapter 2
The Fire Element
Passionate Personality

Light yourself on fire with passion and people will come from miles to watch you burn.

John Wesley

You are Joyful, Passionate, and Charismatic

A person like you with strong Fire energy is very articulate, charismatic and excels at leadership. Your Element commands strong emotional expression and experiences, which can yield satisfying results and personal success. It would be helpful to build your leadership skills and use them to help others fulfill their goals and dreams. Your special ability to motivate others and inspire their passion is a personal asset that will allow you to joyfully connect with those around you.

Compassion is
the Highest Form of Love; Fire Fully Manifested

Compassion the love that emanates from your heart is the vehicle by which you express your Fire energy in its highest form. It helps the world continue to evolve and grow and gives us hope for a better future on earth. To experience peace and serenity within yourself, you must channel your Fire energy into expressions of kindness, compassion and generosity.

Fire People
Have an Eye for Detail

Of all the Elemental types, Fire people are the quickest studies. You are artistic, creative and have an eye for detail. You are also driven, ambitious, and persistent. Conversely, you have a tendency to become frustrated when you are thwarted in any way. Cultivate patience, break down your goals into small, easy to complete tasks and be your own best cheerleader to keep yourself on track.

You've Got the Power
of Persuasion

Fire people can be tremendously powerful and charismatic. Persuasion comes naturally to you. As a Fire Elemental type, you are able to express feelings that move and inspire. Your enthusiasm is infectious, and you connect effortlessly with others. However, you may also be vulnerable to criticism and have your feelings hurt easily. Criticism is like throwing logs on a fire, it will only fuel your passion flame. Welcome it!

Your Heart Energy Network

Fire Element is represented in the human body by the heart network. It is said that Fire people literally feel in their hearts. According to Chinese medicine, the heart houses the spirit, and because the heart and spirit are inseparable, one of your many attributes is intuition. You can sense other's pain instinctively and feel empathy towards them. Not surprisingly, as a high-energy Fire person, you have a tendency to develop cardiac or circulation problems, high blood pressure and anxiety.

You Are Easily Stimulated
and Excitable

When your Fire energy is out of balance, you may be over-stimulated, excited, and lose attention to details. Your need for excitement can drive you to search for other means of stimulation, potentially causing you to become addicted or dependent in unhealthy ways. Because of your need for acknowledgement and validation, you can easily slip into co-dependency. You need to learn how to be vulnerable without giving up emotional independence.

Find Your
Natural Happiness

As a Fire Element person whose emotions color your reality, you need to learn to be objective and analytical in order to make wise decisions. Remember that unguided passion is potentially destructive, can be overwhelming to others, and damaging to yourself. It is important for you as a Fire person to control heavy demands and pressures, and to find your natural happiness ... your own healthy fun, laughter and joy.

Red is Your Color

Red is the primary color of the Fire Element, although pink and purple are sometimes included in the mix. In China, red is the most auspicious of all colors, while in the west, valentines are often red and heart shaped. The color red enlivens, excites and exudes celebratory energy that connects people's hearts in love and laughter both expressions of the Fire Element.

Stay Connected
and Avoid Isolation

If your Fire energy is weak, you may feel "blah," forgetful
or anxious, and have difficulty sleeping. In other words,
you may become depressed. You are naturally sociable,
so it is important that you not become isolated from
friends and family. There are always organizations
or clubs to join if you are in a new situation or
environment; you just need to make the effort.

Smile and Laugh
'Cause it Lights Your Fire

To be true to your Fire nature, you need a reason to smile, to laugh and to experience joy that will engender strong, loving feelings for yourself and for others. If you are having difficulty learning to give and receive love, adopting a pet can help you better understand the meaning of unconditional love. Laughter also produces nitric oxide, a neurochemical that dilates blood vessels and is good for your heart and circulation.

Let Your Intuition
Shine Through

Of all the Elements, you have the easiest access to your spirit. However, if you allow yourself to get so caught up in your emotions that you cannot see clearly, you will block your own intuition. It is very important for you to cultivate spiritual clarity through meditation, chi gong and tai chi, since intuition is the way that your spirit communicates with your conscious mind, giving you information that is hidden for most other types of people.

Resilient Ego
is Cultivated from Self Love

As a Fire person, you are sociable and articulate, but, because you also possess a strong ego, it is possible that you have a difficult time getting along with others. Cultivate a healthy love for yourself. This does not mean narcissism, but rather, something akin to parental love—a kind, compassionate, firm love that is not self-indulgent. This will help you to develop a healthy, resilient ego.

Don't Get Tripped Up
by Idealism

Your perfectionism and idealism can also be obstacles to positive change. As a Fire personality, you may find it difficult to deal with change; be it a change in time zone, environment, temperature, or even a change in the people around you. Cut yourself and others some slack. There is really no perfection in life, just the process of continuous improvement.

Uplift Your Spirit
With Beauty

When your Fire energy is in balance, you should feel robustly healthy and passionate. If you are out of balance, however, you may be anxious, uninspired and apathetic. Your heart spirit responds to beauty, so you may find that a little distraction, such as taking a walk around a pretty neighborhood, looking at beautiful images, or listening to upbeat music, can help to lift your spirit.

Fire Element
Herbal Formula

The herbal formulation for Fire Element promotes a passionate, joyful and enthusiastic spirit by supporting a healthy heart energy network. This also nurtures the brain and the circulation. The Fire Element formula is infused with ginseng—the king of all herbs—traditionally used as a heart tonic that enlivens one's passion whilst keeping the spirit calm; ginkgo, known to support healthy memory and circulation; and Schisandra berry, to arouse joy, ease anguish and encourage peaceful sleep.

Chapter 3
The Earth Element
Caring Personality

You carry Mother Earth within you. She is not outside of you. Mother Earth is not just your environment. When we recognize the virtues, the talent, the beauty of Mother Earth, something is born in us, some kind of connection, love is born.

Thich Nhat Hanh

You Are Caring, Empathetic
and Nurturing

Earth Element persons tend to be caring, empathetic and nurturing. Like the earth's bounty that sustains all lives, you express your Earth nature through kindness and concerns for those around you. Like a mother who nurtures her children with unconditional love, you possess the natural desire to tend to others. You seek first to understand, and are therefore empathetic to people's suffering and misfortune.

There's Something
Easygoing About You

The nature of Earth does not discriminate. It embraces all under the sky. Likewise, you too, are diplomatic, cooperative and easygoing. You derive satisfaction from making others happy and are well liked due to your agreeable nature. You tend to be laidback but reliable. You respond to calls for help. People value your helpful personality and consider you a valuable member of the team.

You are a BFF
(Best Friend Forever)

Earth Element people possess protective, dependable
and loyal properties—traits that make you a desirable
friend. You are fiercely protective of those you care
about and love, those who are vulnerable and feeble,
and those who simply ask help of you. You are a good
friend who can be counted on, in good times and in bad,
rain or shine.

Reaping
What You Have Sown

Earth Element is associated with late summer before the cooling autumn, at the beginning of harvest. Earth energy is manifested as slowing down and gathering in; reaping what you have sown, both in nature and in life. As an Earth person, you are likely to be well grounded and sympathetic; a nurturing peacemaker who attempts to maintain harmony.

You May be Generous
to a Fault

As the Earth is generous and bountiful, so too are you sometimes to a fault. You have a tendency to overcompensate for what is lacking in others. You can easily give more than you receive and this may lead to your interpersonal relationships becoming out of balance. Because you are a natural caregiver, you may find that you feel drained and exhausted to the point of feeling used or resentful.

Overindulgence Leads
to Overt Compassion

Your willingness to overindulge others may lead them to a sense of entitlement. They may become like spoiled children, unable to reciprocate the love and care that you have so thoughtfully provided for them. You like being in the role of a savior, but when you are overextended and depleted, you can become unhappy, resentful and unfulfilled. When compassion becomes overindulgence, it is called "overt compassion." This obviously results in a negative outcome. It is important for you to create healthy boundaries without feeling guilty, so that others do not abuse your natural generosity.

Don't Worry,
Accept Change

It is important for you to be aware that Earth people
tend to be worriers. It is quite possible for you to
get stuck in a circle of thoughts. Your tendency to
ruminate can make you feel very anxious, since neither
ruminating nor over-thinking solves problems. You
need to learn to trust, accept that change is normal and
constant, and know that as long as you are centered and
balanced, you will always find a way to overcome.

Natural Born
Peacemaker

The Earth Element is aligned with the harvest season.
It is the balanced center between the Yang Elements
of Wood and Fire, and the Yin Elements of Metal and
Water. Earth is the season of gathering; the pivotal
central Element that is the transition between the Yang
seasons of planting and growing, and the Yin seasons of
cooling and hibernation. This balance of Yin and Yang is
why you are a natural born mediator and peacemaker.

Earth Is
Assimilation

Earth energy corresponds to the process of assimilation in nature, and to the digestive system in the human body. Earth Element people tend to be strong and solidly built. If your Element is out of balance, however, you may be emaciated, malnourished, or, on the opposite end of the scale, obese. Your Element is prone to eating disorders and digestive problems, so it is important for you to avoid excessive indulgence or obsessions with foods, habits or objects.

You Need to Feel the Earth
Move Under Your Feet

The Earth Element features the ability to embrace and accept, something that does not come as easily to other personalities. You can leverage this natural advantage in your spiritual growth, but always remember that you need physical movement as well. You literally need to feel the earth move under your feet. Practicing tai chi, chi gong, walking or hiking will mobilize your energy and help you avoid becoming stagnant or unhealthy.

Little Yield
From Excessive Worry

An out of balance Earth Element can be a meddler or
an obsessive worrier. The excessive rumination is akin
to disrupting the cycle of planting, nourishing, and
then harvesting a crop. When there is a disruption
and imbalance in nature, there will be very little yield.
Likewise if you worry excessively, there is very little
productive outcome because all the activity takes place
in your head, with little or no manifested result. If your
energy is out of balance, you may also be lacking in
sympathy, insatiably needy, or find it difficult to ask
others for help.

Yellow
is Your Color

Different colors project the energetic quality of each Element. In the case of the Earth Element, yellow is the primary color, although shades of brown, orange, ochre and gold are also included. Warm metals like gold, brass and copper are more natural for your Earth energy, than silver, steel or chrome. Studies show that different colors affect humans subconsciously, and yellow invokes the generous, abundant and benevolent nature of the Earth Element.

You Need Regular Cycles
and Rhythm

Just as the earth works in regular cycles, so do you,
as an Earth person, need to set aside regular times
for sleep, meals, play and work. You need to strike
a balance between rest and work in order to avoid
exhausting or stressing yourself to the point of illness.
In addition, you may find that you benefit from stepping
back from emotional people, and emotional subjects, in
order to protect your mind and your energy.

Healthy Earth
Means Healthy Digestion

In Chinese medicine, Earth energy oversees nourishment not only of the body but also of the spirit. When your Earth element is in balance, you are a happy, healthy, loving and giving human being. But if you are out of balance, you have a tendency toward stomach and digestive issues. Indigestion, bloating, and sugar highs and lows are common in your element. So, Earth people, beware! Diabetes could be lurking around the corner.

Earth Element
Herbal Formula

The herbal formulation for the Earth Element encourages caring, stability, empathy and contentment of the spirit by supporting a healthy stomach energy network. The Earth Element formula is infused with Codonopsis root, traditionally used to promote healthy digestion and nurture an abundance of energy; Longan fruit—also called dragon eyes—known for its properties of fostering empathy and contentment of spirit; and Polygonatum root, which provides grounding and stability of one's presence.

Chapter 4
The Metal Element
Methodical Personality

Lead will play its role until the world has no further need for lead; and then lead will have to turn itself into gold. That's what alchemists do. They show that when we strive to become better than we are, everything around us becomes better, too.

Paulo Coelho

You Are Intellectual
and Analytical

Your Metal Element personality tends to be intellectual, inquisitive and analytical. You naturally excel at taking reams of information that may overwhelm others, and organizing it into systematized and accessible arrangements. You are skilled at transformation, able to take seemingly unrelated parts and assemble them into a unified whole. Additionally, you effortlessly analyze and make sense of complex problems.

You Are High Achieving
and Perfectionistic

Metal Element persons are rational, organized, detail oriented, methodical, and perfectionistic. The positive side of your perfectionism is that you are a high achiever who enjoys recognition and approval. You enjoy taking time and doing things right, with attention to detail. There is logic to your thought process, which is expressed in your highly rational intellect that is both efficient and effective.

Reflect, Open
and Transform

Transformation is both the nature and symbol of the
Metal Element. You have a natural ability to look
back and reflect, which is why your Metal personality
is drawn to spiritual quests. Your transformation
begins with peeling back the protective layers of your
personality. Once you understand and acknowledge who
you are, you will discover your potential and ultimately,
actualize your goals.

Autumn Is the Season
of the Metal Element

Metal energy marks the end of the growing season, when the earth begins to turn inward. Leaves and crops give forth a final burst of color, the air becomes crisp and we begin to think of the upcoming winter, of hearth and home, fallow fields and quietude. The energy of the Metal Element is manifested as cooling and contracting. As the leaves fall from the tree, you as a Metal person, probably experience some sadness. If your Elemental energy is healthy, you are able to acknowledge sadness, but at the same time allow the leaves to fall and fertilize the earth so that the cycle of life can move forward.

You Have
a Strong Personality

It is necessary for you as a Metal Element person to let go of negativity in order to enjoy your strength and power. Your element has a strong personality, like the natural immunity that defends you from harmful people and elements. And because you are motivated by self-improvement, you are likely to be a very high achiever.

Don't Give in to Paralysis
by Analysis

Your optimistic outlook, curious nature, and ability to entertain myriad possibilities can lead you to excessive deliberation and analysis. This can cause you to change your mind often and spread yourself too thin, thus becoming scattered, unfocused and paralyzed. And because you are so good at what you do, you may find yourself becoming overextended. When your Metal Element is in balance, you are organized, accomplished, inspired, and at peace with yourself and with others. As in all matters, and all existence, balance is key.

Watch Out for Rigidity
and Inflexibility

As a Metal personality, you tend to be cautious, conservative, and good at planning. However, when things don't go according to your plan, try to remember that your criticism and rigidity often follow closely behind. The downside of your Element, is that as a perfectionist, you can be rigid and inflexible and may have difficulty moving beyond your self-imposed rules and boundaries. Cultivate flexibility—don't be a stiff, chrome bumper but a flexible one that can withstand life's bumps and scratches.

White Is the Color
of Metal Element

Color is energy that emanates from the visible light spectrum and affects human physiology and mood. White is the primary color of the Metal Element. This also includes off-white, eggshell, pale beige, light grey, silver and metallic and reflective properties of any color. The energy of the whites is pure and reflective, but sometimes feels cold, distant and unforgiving. Mix in a light shade or hue of other colors to become more accessible and welcoming.

Metal Element Manifests
as the Lung Energy Network

Metal Element is represented in the human body by the lung energy network. It is associated with the defensive systems of the body, which includes the immunity, the intestinal track, and the skin. The lungs are the body's defense against pathogens, so Metal Elemental types whose energy gets weak or unbalanced are prone to respiratory conditions like shortness of breath, stuffiness, sinusitis, allergy, asthma, colds and flu. Other signs of Metal Element imbalance include cough, dry skin, constipation, colitis, skin breakouts, fatigue, chills, a weak voice, exhaustion, sadness and self-destructive behaviors.

Cultivate Tolerance
and Acceptance

If you are an unbalanced, opinionated, inflexible Metal person, it is quite possible that you subscribe to long-held principles and beliefs. As a perfectionist, you can be very critical, both of yourself and of others. Cultivating tolerance and acceptance of your own attributes and those of others is a very important aspect of bringing your Element into balance. Whether you perceive these attributes to be positive or negative, your acceptance of them will stop you from being critical and help you embrace change and challenge.

Open Your Chest
and Take in a New Breath

Your tendency is to close yourself off and to keep your emotions hidden. When you suppress your feelings, it's akin to your chest being closed tight by a large leather strap. You are unable to take in a new breath of fresh oxygen. This deprives you of life and new possibilities. You may find it difficult to transform your sadness into something positive, and to find acceptance, but the act of letting go throws open the gates, and creates opportunities for the future. This ultimately allows you to find and experience joy.

The Alchemy
of Self-Actualization

The transformation that is part of your nature relates back to ancient alchemists, who experimented with refining base metals in attempts to transform them into gold. The challenge of the Metal personality is self-discovery, followed by cultivation and self-actualization. This is, of course, the ideal scenario, with a person who is on the path of spiritual growth. Transformation can be accomplished with self-cultivation which is incremental improvements of yourself in order to reach the gold of a balanced Metal element.

Exercise Balance
and Appropriate Action

Metal people tend to be cautious and conservative. These traits cut both ways. Sometimes it pays to be conservative, while other times you might miss opportunities for growth and personal gains. First, accept where you are in life. That will stop the critical self-talk that takes place in your head. Second, write down potential outcomes for each extreme scenarios on both margins of a piece of paper, then draw a line connecting them. Along the line write down potential outcomes between the two extremes. Third, deliberate and assess the risks associated with each scenario and decide what you are comfortable with. Finally you may allow yourself to exercise and take calculated and appropriate risks.

Lift Your Spirit
and Bring Love Into Your Life

Since you tend to be a reserved personality who may tend toward sadness, mood-lifting activities like music, dance, singing and chanting would be helpful to you. Laughter is your antidote and so is creating connections. Adopting a pet may be a way of lifting your spirits and bringing love into your life, as is cultivating friendships, both old and new.

Metal Element
Herbal Formula

The herbal formulation for the Metal Element stimulates strength and endurance, uplifts sorrow, and supports healthy immunity and the lung energy network. The Metal Element formula is infused with honeysuckle. This is traditionally used to strengthen the lung energy network, and clear one's emotional burden. Ligustrum fruit is well studied for its immune support and protective properties, and Lycium or Gojiberry is known as an endurance tonic and also contains potent antioxidants.

Chapter 5
The Water Element
Wise Personality

The water in a vessel is sparkling; the water in the sea is dark. The small truth has words, which are clear; the great truth has great silence.

Rabindranath Tagore

You Are Confident,
Enduring and Deep

As a Water Element person, you are a powerful force with a great capacity for endurance. Your strong will and confidence springs not from an excess of ego, but from a deeply-rooted connection to your very being, your Jing or essence, your foundation, your source. There's depth to the quality of your being, like that of the deep blue sea—it is primal and mysterious.

You Use Your Wisdom
to Elevate Others

You are a born teacher, leader and visionary. You have a gift for learning and a natural ability for using your wisdom, knowledge and power in order to elevate those around you. Your nature, like that of the Elemental Water, is buoyant, and supports your family and friends. The Water temperament naturally embraces myriad substances as it permeates all of life and makes its way to the sea. Others are attracted to you for your wise counsel because you, like the crystal clear, reflecting lake, enable those who seek it to see what they cannot see on their own.

Water Contains
the Essence of Life

The Water Element is, energetically speaking, the time
of winter. It is a time of pulling back to the root, also
known as the Jing, the basic essence of life. "Jing"
describes the substance and function of DNA, our
essence—the genetic material that contains the stored
memories of millions of years of evolution. It is our Jing
that enables life to be renewed and to begin again. We
store energy in the winter so that rejuvenation and
rebirth can take place in the spring. Winter is a time of
rest when we build our reserves for the seasons ahead.
Likewise, your Element expresses the foundation for
rebirth, reinvention and re-imagination of your life.

Don't Let Fear
Stop You in Your Flow

The Water Element is associated with a strong survival instinct that is motivated by fear. It is quite possible for you to overwork to the point of exhaustion, or to become so anxious that you become emotionally paralyzed. Your fear can be balanced with education and knowledge, which will, in turn, help you to understand the difference between risk and reward. That way, like Water flowing in nature, you can always find a way around blockages.

Water Element
and the Kidney-Adrenal Energy Network

Water regulates the kidneys' energy network. This includes the bladder, reproductive organs and hormonal system. Thus, Water people are susceptible to urinary, hormonal and reproductive problems. The kidney adrenals are particularly vulnerable to stress, and that is why it is very important for you to cultivate your essence, your life root source, your Jing—by soaking up the right nutrients, herbs and supplements.

You've Got to Conceive
to Give Birth

Your power as a Water Element person comes from your vision and ability to create or conceive, so it would be wise to look for endeavors that take advantage of your natural imagination, your self-sufficiency and love of learning. The founder of Fat Burger restaurant chain, Lovie Yancey, who was an African American woman trying to start a business in the 1940s, once shared with me the secret to her success. "Honey, you've got to conceive in order to give birth to your dream, baby!" With that unstoppable imagination and unshakeable determination, she launched and succeeded in her business, against all odds.

Your Elemental Colors
Are Blue and Black

As a Water person, you have a strong hidden reservoir
of power, and need an appropriate environment
to support and nourish it. Color encapsulates and
expresses the power of the sun's energy, which has
major impact on all living and nonliving things on our
planet earth. The best colors for nourishing the Water
Element are black or blue, with accents of dark blue and
purple.

When Your Chi Is Strong
Your Spirit Will Soar

Water energy is heavy, and naturally tends to descend, sink or stop moving. This is the reason why Water people have a tendency to feel sad, or to hold rigid opinions that makes others view them as stuck or inflexible. It is important for your energy to move easily and forward in a constructive way ... to go with the flow, so to speak. You can keep your energy light, strong and flowing by meditating, practicing tai chi or chi gong, or engaging in some other sort of regular exercise. When your chi is strong, you will feel and be uplifted—your spirit will soar and you will be able to do what you do best, which is to guide and inspire others.

The Two Sides
of the Water Energy

It is natural for Water energy to have two sides: one side is vulnerable and the other is fearless. When you are tired, and your energy is out of balance, you may feel cautious and unwilling to take risks, even though you are very creative and capable. When balanced, you happily harness your Water energy and unleash a torrent of creativity that's full of confidence and grace.

Potential for Change
Lies Within You

Buried deep within your Element is the seed of the great upward, growing, thrusting energy of yang that bursts through in the spring. This explains why the greatest ability and potential for change lies within Water Element people. Just keep in mind that change, wisely made, requires time and calm contemplation. It's an act of discipline to maintain enduring and consistent flow and change. So take time to prepare and be ready for the opportune moment to unleash your hidden power.

Know When to Advise
and When to Retreat

You are likely to be a dreamer—a reflective, deep
thinker. It is helpful for you to bring your wisdom to
others, but it is important that you do so in a graceful
way. You will learn from experience when it is time to
offer advice, and when it is time to retreat, just like a
quiet brook nourishing all that it touches without the
commotions of a river rapid.

Prioritize
and Let Go

Because you are likely to be highly creative, you may find that you are prone to scattering and overextending yourself. When you are overextended, stressed out and depleted, you will probably lose your ability to make wise decisions. It will be helpful for you to learn to prioritize and let go of that which is not necessary. Likewise, when you are tired, you can become hypersensitive to what you perceive as threatening, which can make you become cautious to the point of being consumed with worry or fear.

Achieve "No Mind"
State of Being

Water is the best able of all the Elements to achieve what in Zen meditation is called "no mind." This is a receptive, open minded, universal awareness. That is why activities that bring ideas from the subconscious to fruition are perfect hobbies for you: drawing, sculpting, writing... just to name a few. It is important for you to cultivate a healthy lifestyle, give yourself time to rest, and nourish yourself so that you can make wise choices and discover your dreams.

Tap Into Guidance
from Your Spirit

Spirituality comes easily to naturally meditative, deep thinking Water people. You understand the true meaning of trust, devotion and forgiveness. As a Water person, it is helpful for you to actively cultivate spiritual faith and robust life-force energy, or chi. You can then tap into guidance from your spirit, and use your energy to manifest your dreams. One way to do this is to ask your spirit for guidance before falling asleep, with queries like, "Dear Divine, Source of All Life please reveal to me my ultimate purpose for my existence and give me the strength to actualize it."

The Water Element
Herbal Formula

The herbal formulation for Water nurtures a receptive, calm and determined spirit by supporting a healthy kidney-adrenals energy network, as well as hormone balance. The Water Element formula is infused with Chinese Wild Yam, traditionally used to enrich Jing and replenish the hormonal reservoir. It also includes Rehmannia root to nourish and boost kidney-adrenal energy, the seat of fertility and vitality, and Achyranthes, known to strengthen the will, stamina and endurance.

Part Two
Your Life

Your Element affects five significant aspects of your life—the health of your mind, body, relationships, career and finances. We simply call these The Five Healths. Throughout your life you will encounter unique opportunities and challenges. Your experiences, decisions and the resulting outcome are invariably shaped by who you are, your Elemental tendencies and the emotional blockages that prevent you from fully actualizing your potential.

Take the example of a Wood Element/Authoritative type, whose type A, driven and impatient personality helps him or her to initiate projects, make tough decisions and get things done on time, and on budget. These qualities are appreciated and often rewarded at work. However, when these traits are pushed to the extreme and the stress and tension become untenable, the health of the mind and body will suffer, sometimes fatally, as with high blood pressure, stroke and heart attacks.

When the Wood Element is kept in balance, the "driven" trait may motivate the person to eat well, meditate, exercise and keep calm. The optimization of one's core Element, and the balancing of all five Elements benefits each of The Five Healths in turn.

Sticking with the example of the Wood Element/ Authoritative type, whose leadership and managerial qualities may help him or her to succeed at work by corralling the team, barking marching orders, and meeting ever increasing performance targets and deadlines, at home his or her spouse may feel belittled, bullied or resentful of the same approach used at work. Essential qualities for success in one area of one's life become liabilities in another. Why does this happen?

Obviously, the commanding and authoritative style of an army general is ill suited in interpersonal relationships with a spouse, children and friends. In fact, it is often the source of conflict and discord in a relationship, and can be prevented by harmonizing the Wood Element and cultivating balance.

The advice given in Chapters 1-5 provides practical solutions for improving your Elemental personality weaknesses, and removing blockages that separate you and your loved ones from experiencing fulfilling relationships. Chapters 6-10 will provide the life context for each element/personality type, and respective tips and solutions for blockage-release, optimizing and balancing. Read on to unlock the secrets of ancient sages that are the foundation for health, happiness and success in your life.

Chapter 6
Physical Health

We know a great deal more about the causes of physical disease than we do about the causes of physical health.

M. Scott Peck

You Are Responsible
for Your Own Health

Comprehensive physical health means being disease-free as well as having abundant energy and vitality. We take our health for granted until something goes wrong. Illness can guide us to change our life habits for the better, but this is not a pleasant way of being reminded. If we can focus on learning how to take care our bodies and understanding the integral function of body, mind and spirit, then we can restore ourselves with innate healing power, or prevent illness before it occurs. The basics to improving physical health and preventing illness include: a balanced diet and healthy nutrition, good sleep and plenty of rest, appropriate exercise, a clean environment, and the use of herbal supplements for Elemental support and healing. You are responsible for your own health and you can make a difference.

Self-Care Is Essential
to Good Health and Lower Costs

Healthcare in America is in crisis. The U.S. health care system is the most expensive in the world but studies consistently show the U.S. underperforms relative to other countries. Most troubling—the U.S. fails to achieve better health outcomes, with a lower quality of care and efficiency than most industrialized countries. While health care reform has expanded access for those formerly uninsured, the ultimate challenge will be delivering wellness to the population, while maintaining reasonable costs. The new focus of healthcare organizations is on empowering self-care. By giving the responsibility back to each individual we can finally begin to realize a healthier society.

Wood
Element

According to Chinese medicine, the Wood Element is expressed in the human body as the liver energy network, which includes the liver and gallbladder, the nervous system, and the tendons and ligaments that link all the bones and muscles together into an interconnected whole.

The liver energy network's main job is neutralizing and eliminating toxins that come into the body through what you eat, drink, breathe, and touch. The liver takes all the waste and toxins and converts them into bile, which is then stored in the gallbladder and eliminated each time you consume fats. If the liver is overwhelmed by too many toxins, such as alcohol, contamination or heavy metals (mercury in fish, for example, or medication), its ability to eliminate toxins becomes impaired. When toxins build up in the body, it can lead to many unpleasant symptoms and functional imbalances, including fatigue, memory loss, weight gain, flank pain, abdominal bloating, gas, jaundice, inflammation, allergies, and more.

Detox Solutions:

- Upon rising each morning for one week, squeeze one lemon into 12 ounces of hot water and drink to activate the liver's detoxification process.

- Take two capsules of probiotics on an empty stomach to balance the gut biome.

- Drink eight ounces of vegetable juices, twice a day in between meals, to increase antioxidant vitamins for one week.

- Take Wood Element herbal formula to support cleansing and detoxification (see resources)

- Eliminate all animal products for one week.

- Eliminate all dairy, alcohol, caffeine, sugar, deep fried, fatty, processed and refined foods.

- Add coconut oil, avocado oil and walnut oil to your diet.

- Practice Wood Element Chi Gong daily (see Appendix).

Stress Affects the Nervous System
Especially the Autonomic

Remember that stress comes along with change. If your Wood Element is unbalanced, the stress will cause your liver energy to become blocked, or toxic. A careless diet, endless stress, recreational drugs and alcohol weaken liver energy and create a brittle nervous system. When your Wood Element is imbalanced, you might experience headaches, eye problems, dizziness, vertigo, tinnitus, numbness, tingling, tremors, stiffness and pain, depression, mania, anger outbursts, memory and cognitive decline. When a severe imbalance occurs, seizures, stroke, and paralysis may also occur. Additionally, the autonomic nervous system regulates biorhythms of the body such as sleep cycle, intestinal peristalsis, heart rate and blood pressure. Therefore, with extreme imbalances, insomnia, irregular bowel movement, irregular heart rate and high blood pressure can occur.

Calming Solutions:

- Keep a daily journal to offload all feelings, especially anger, resentment, despair, isolation and frustration.

- Begin a nightly meditation practice before bedtime to clear stress and tension. Try *Meditation for Stress Release.* (See Appendix)

- Walk 10,000 steps daily to release pent up liver energy.

- Walk barefoot on grass to discharge destructive positively charged ions—such as carbon dioxide, smog and electronic pollution.

Wood Imbalance Weakens
Tendons and Ligaments

When the authoritative personality of the Wood
Element is imbalanced, the connective tissues, such
as ligaments and tendons, become prone to being
tight, injured or compromised. This leads to joint or
muscle pain, tendonitis, and dislocations, which can
greatly limit range of motion and movement. Ironically,
movement is precisely what you need to prevent energy
stagnation but be sure to be gentle.

Restoring Solutions:

- Warm up and stretch upon waking and before beginning any exercise.

- Use the Foundation Practice to prevent injury (see Appendix).

- Warm up with therapeutic heat, such as infrared sauna.

- Ice down after exercise

- Take a joint health herbal formula to support the soft tissue around joints. See Resources.

- Get acupuncture treatments or apply self acupressure to the tendons and ligaments to speed healing.

Eating Right for the Wood Element/
Liver Energy Network

Of all the Elemental types, as a Wood person you are the most vulnerable to toxins. It is in your best interest to severely limit or completely eliminate alcohol, cigarettes, recreational drugs, most pain relievers and caffeine. You need to search out clean, simple foods that are supportive to the liver: dark leafy greens, cruciferous vegetables, brightly colored fruits and healthy fats that are found in whole grains, legumes, raw nuts and seeds.

Sour foods stimulate digestion and encourage the production of bile. Wood Elemental types tend to enjoy sour foods such as citrus fruit, grapefruit juice, lemon and limeade, as well as products like pickles, kimchi, miso and sauerkraut. Drink plenty of herbal teas, such as the Ancient Treasures Tea, that contain powerful liver cleansers like chamomile, peppermint or dandelion. Clean air and pure water are especially important for you. Avoid pesticides and pollutants of all sorts in order to remain healthy.

Good nutrition will allow you to have clarity of mind, creativity and focus.

Fire
Element

According to Chinese medicine, Fire Element relates to the heart energy network, which includes the heart, vascular system, small intestine, mood and brain—particularly the part that governs the conscious mind.

Not surprisingly, as a high-energy Fire Elemental type, you have a tendency to develop cardiac or circulation problems and high blood pressure. Typical symptoms of heart conditions include shortness of breath, palpitations, dizziness, chest pain or discomfort, and tingling or numbness radiating down the left arm. However, some people with heart disease do not display any symptoms until it's too late. Therefore it's important to assess your heart health regularly with your doctor, especially if you have a family history of heart disease.

Energizing Solutions:

- Practice Fire Element Chi Gong daily (see Appendix).

- Do at least 30 minutes of cardiovascular exercise, such as fast walking, running or biking for 30 minutes at least four times a week.

- Take Fire Element herbal formula to support heart energy (see Resources).

- Cut out all animal fats and add olive oil, hemp oil and flax seed oil into your diet.

- Lose weight, and keep your BMI (body mass index) below 25 (see Appendix).

Fire Element's
Passionate Personality and Mood

Interestingly, the small intestine is part of the heart energy network in Chinese medicine, and it turns out that about 90% of serotonin is produced and found in your intestines. A healthy level of serotonin has positive impact on your mood, sense of peace and sleep. Therefore, intestinal health is critical to heart health.

Calming Solutions:

- Practice meditation for stress release daily (see Appendix).

- Drink Ancient Treasures Tea for its calming and soothing properties (see Resources).

- Try to belly laugh for at least 15 minutes every day, from watching comedies for example.

- Throw a party and invite your friends over.

- Eat dark chocolate with at least 70% cacao and low sugar.

Eating Right for the Fire Element/
Heart Energy Network

As a Fire Elemental type, you tend to enjoy bitter foods like dark chocolate, aperitifs, craft beers, olives, bitter greens, coffee and black tea. In Chinese medicine, the explanation is straightforward and simple—bitter foods cool excess Fire. Fire is the hottest and most yang of all the elements, and tends to produce the most heat. This is why you will do well with a light menu that limits alcohol and avoids excessively spicy or greasy foods. Your constitution will benefit from cooling foods like melons, salads and citrus.

Because you enjoy bitter tastes, you might want to make salads with spinach, arugula, dandelion greens or radicchio. Add some crisp, sliced Asian pears, sprinkle with sunflower seeds and serve with a delightful lemon vinaigrette dressing. You get the idea—your meals need be light, cooling and heart-healthy.

Earth
Element

According to Chinese medicine, Earth Element is associated with the spleen-stomach energy network, which includes the digestive and metabolic systems, as well as the information processing activities of the mind. Since digestive and metabolic functions are so critical for energy and vitality, weakness in the Earth Element will manifest as low energy, brain fog, and an imbalanced immune system.

Because nourishment depends upon healthy digestion, it is not surprising that a person with unbalanced Earth energy has a tendency toward stomach and digestive issues. The Spleen-Stomach Energy Network is highly reactive to dampness and mold, both internally and externally. Internally, dampness comes from foods that encourage overgrowth of yeast and fungus, such as foods high in sugar. Other culprits include cow dairy products, refined grains (pastries and pastas), alcohol and deep fried, fatty foods. Externally, dampness comes from prolonged exposure to mold. Indigestion, bloating, burping, nausea, vomiting, flatulence, ulcers, diarrhea, or constipation may be common with your Element. Excessive mucus and sinus allergies may also be a result of dampness affecting your immune function.

Digestive Solutions:

- Eat regular meals, in moderate amounts, seated rather than standing, in a calm environment.

- Chew your food well and enjoy it, rather than gulping and rushing off.

- Eat cooked rather than raw ingredients.

- Take Earth Element herbal formula and probiotics to support healthy digestion and gut function (see Resources).

- Avoid cow dairy, gluten-containing grains like wheat, barley and rye, sugar, including most fruits, and yeast-containing foods such as pastries, beer and wine.

- Practice Earth Element Chi Gong to restore healthy gut peristalsis (see Appendix).

- Go for a stroll after each meal and massage your abdomen clockwise 100 circles.

Metabolic Function
Is Earth's Transformation

Your metabolism is intricately linked to the Earth energy of transformation, which when imbalanced, can lead to anorexia or becoming overweight. Muscle formation and maintenance is also under the domain of the spleen-stomach energy network, so poor muscle tone may be a tendency. Earth people are also susceptible to eating disorders, sugar highs and lows, and food cravings, especially for sweets. So, for you, Earth types, diabetes is a concern.

Metabolic Solutions:

- Eat quinoa, amaranth, whole oats, buckwheat, brown rice, sweet potato, yams, squash and pumpkins as your starch.

- Eat five small meals a day to help stimulate metabolism.

- Add herbs and spices into your diet such as rosemary, thyme, ginger, cinnamon and fennel.

- Avoid moldy environments. If this is not possible, get a dehumidifier.

- Drink Ancient Treasures Tea or cinnamon tea to help sugar balance (see Resources).

- Do toning exercise 3–4 times a week, such as tai chi, yoga or light weight training.

- Practice merry-go-round circle walking for 15 minutes daily (see Appendix).

Eating Right for the Earth Element/
Stomach-Spleen Energy System

Earth's flavor is sweet, and most Earths enjoy sweet foods of all sorts. In order to be healthy and balanced, you must learn to strengthen your energy by practicing moderation and regular dietary habits. The most fortifying foods for you are dense and tightly packed fruits and vegetables such as sweet potatoes, carrots, Brussels sprouts, persimmons and cherries. In Chinese medicine, stomach energy flourishes with regularity and moderation, so of all the Elemental types, you need to eat regular meals, in moderate amounts, seated rather than standing, in a calm environment, while appreciating the beauty, taste and source of what is on your plate.

Your energy benefits from cooked rather than raw ingredients. Food and drink for you are healthiest served at room temperature or warm, rather than icy cold or scalding hot. In order to encourage digestion, it is important for you to chew your food well, and enjoy it, rather than gulping and rushing off to some other activity. In moderation, gluten-free grains are highly healing and energizing for you, as are yams and sweet potatoes. Most meats, fish, beans and nuts are also considered to be sweet foods that will benefit your energy, as long as they are eaten in reasonable quantities.

Metal
Element

According to Chinese medicine, the Metal Element is associated with the lung energy network, which encompasses the respiratory system including the sinuses, skin and the immune system.

The lungs are the body's defense against pathogens, so Metal types of people are prone to respiratory conditions such as stuffiness, shortness of breath, fatigue, sinusitis, allergies, asthma, colds and flu.

Enhancement Solutions:

- Practice breathing exercises daily. Breathe fresh air deeply and slowly, and count to 10 on every inhale and exhale for 5–10 minutes.

- Take the Metal Element herbal formula to support healthy lung energy network (see Resources).

- Wash your hands often. Avoid touching your face, especially your nose, mouth and eyes.

- Incorporate garlic, oregano and anise into your diet to harness nature's antiviral and antibacterial power.

- Practice Metal Element Chi Gong to strengthen your body's self-defense (see Appendix).

- Take probiotics supplement and eat fermented foods such as sauerkraut, miso and kimchi.

Lung Energy Network
Governs the Skin

The lung energy network governs the skin, the largest organ in your body. Just like the lungs, your skin breathes and absorbs whatever it contacts, eliminating wastes and toxins through perspiration. Signs of Metal imbalance include cough, dry skin, constipation, colitis, and skin rashes including eczema, psoriasis and acne breakouts.

Protective Solutions:

- Buy natural shampoo and body wash without harsh chemicals.

- Use the renewing cleanser, radiant day cream and regenerating night cream, which contain Chinese herbs and extracts of pearl powder that gently cleanse and nourish your skin (see Resources).

- Drink at least 8–10 glasses of purified water daily.

- Eat at least eight servings of fruits and vegetables. One serving is equal to about ½ cup.

- Get a filter for your shower head to get rid of skin-harming chlorine and other chemicals.

Eating Right for the Metal Element/
Lung Energy Network

Pungent foods that move energy outward and upward appeal to you as a Metal person. Pungency refers to hot and spicy foods with powerful, strong, penetrating flavors. A small amount is good for the lung energy network, including garlic, onions of all sorts and chili peppers. Other pungent foods include ginger, celery, coriander, fennel, spearmint, horseradish, fennel, anise, dill, radish leaves, sweet peppers, turnips, mustard leaf, cinnamon, tangerine peel, kumquats, mustard seed and wine. Additionally, basil and rosemary are pungent, as are parsley, coriander, cloves and cayenne.

Fruits that requiring peeling support your health: particularly citrus, bananas and mangoes eaten during the harvest season. Interestingly, many of your healthiest foods are white, such as onions, garlic, cauliflower, turnips and parsnips. During the cool and cold seasons of the year, root vegetables like potatoes, yams, turnips and carrots are perfect for strengthening your Elemental energy; they are easy to prepare, and become deliciously caramelized when roasted in the oven.

Water
Element

According to Chinese medicine, Water Element is associated with the kidney-adrenal energy network, which encompasses the urinary system, adrenal function, and the hormonal and reproductive systems.

Your urinary system is responsible for ridding the body of toxins and maintaining critical water, mineral and electrolyte balance. When your kidney-adrenal Network is off balance you may be prone to frequent urination, incontinence, difficulty urinating, bladder and urinary track infections, kidney stones, low blood pressure, dehydration, water retention, bloating, and dizziness.

Balancing Solutions:

- Drink diluted cranberry and/or tart cherry juice to keep your urinary track acidic, excrete uric acid and to prevent infections.

- Keep track of your water and electrolyte balance. This means that when you drink a lot of water, don't forget to eat potassium-rich foods, like banana and oranges, and add a little more salt to your diet.

- Take the Water Element herbal supplement to support kidney-adrenal Energies (see Resources)

- Take a walk by a stream, lake or ocean to connect with Water energy.

- Practice Kegel exercises to strengthen your bladder sphincter muscles.

Stress Is Your
Achilles Heel

The kidney-adrenal energy network is particularly vulnerable to stress, and that is why it is very important for you to cultivate your essence, your life root source or Jing. When your energy is depleted or out of balance, you may perceive danger, become fearful or go into survival mode when the circumstances do not necessarily require this, and you have great difficulty moving forward. As a result, imbalance of your Water Element may predispose you to nervousness, anxiety, depression, difficulty sleeping, shortness of breath, high blood pressure, hair loss, memory loss, poor focus and concentration, and pain in your back, knees and heels.

Relaxing Solutions:

- Practice Meditation for Stress Release (see Appendix).

- Learn Water Element Chi Gong to support your stress tolerance (see Appendix).

- Take Water Element herbal supplement to restore your kidney-adrenal balance (see Resources).

- Enjoy a hot bath infused with essential oils, like lavender.

- Lean your back against a tree and feel your body becoming deeply rooted and unshakable.

- Reframe your situation to give you a better perspective, and therefore, adjust your negative reactions and stressful response.

Water Element Is the Root
of Vitality and Fertility

Water energy is the time of winter, of pulling back to the root, or, Jing, the basic essence of life. Jing describes the substance and function of DNA, our essence, the genetic material that contains the stored memories of millions of years of evolution. Buried deep within your Element is the seed of the great fertility energy that bursts through in the spring. This is why when the kidney-adrenal energy network is off balance, you may have a tendency to develop low vitality, erectile dysfunction, menstrual irregularity, infertility and bone loss.

Rejuvenation Solutions:

- Get plenty of sleep, go to bed early and sleep late.

- Practice Water Element Chi Gong to strengthen your kidney-adrenal energy Network (see Appendix).

- Increase your intake of healthy fats, such as virgin coconut oil, walnut oil, avocado oil and flax seed oil.

- Take Water Element herbal supplements to support healthy hormonal balance and fertility (see Resources).

- Stay warm by avoiding air conditioning and ice cold drinks and by wearing plenty of clothes.

- Eat a plant based, moderate protein diet to protect against calcium lost from high protein diet.

- Drink bone broth cooked with black beans to nourish the bones with calcium.

Eating Right for the Water Element/
Kidney-Adrenal Energy Network

The flavor of both yin and Water is salty. Salt moves energy downward and inward, stimulates appetite and improves digestion. Salty foods include seaweed and many Asian sauces. Barley and millet are considered to be both salty and sweet. Our kidneys require a small amount of salt in order to properly regulate water metabolism, but as we all know, too much salt can damage them, not to mention increase blood pressure in susceptible people.

Black, blue and purple foods support the kidneys and strengthen the yin. Examples of foods that nourish the Water Element include blueberries, blackberries, dark grapes, eggplant, wild rice, blue corn and purple potatoes. You will probably find that your constitution does best with cooked foods, and complex carbohydrates. The sorts of dishes that are healthy for you are made with whole grains, peas, squash, beans and root vegetables like potatoes, carrots and parsnips. Warming spices are helpful in strengthening your energy—think "cinnamon and spice, and everything nice." That is a perfect combination for you!

Chapter 7
Mind Health

The Integral Mind
Intellect, Emotions and Intuition

Mind health is about cultivating the integral mind, which is the balance of your intellect, emotions and intuition. Most people overly develop their intellectual minds and neglect to nurture their emotional and spiritual minds. Achieving mind health increases your effectiveness in life by building on your intuition and creativity.

Mind health is also about transcending emotions and resolving any entanglements. The mind is in charge of managing all your affairs and actions. Emotions arise when your expectations and belief systems conflict with reality, and you find yourself unable to reconcile the gap. Cultivating the unconditioned mind will help you respond to any situation appropriately, so that you are free to move beyond your old emotional and behavioral patterns.

Attain a Calm
and Peaceful Mind

Your mind health is the key to your body health, as the
mind orchestrates all aspects of your worldly life. Your
physical health, in turn, greatly impacts your mind,
thoughts and emotions. Spiritual health is also largely
dependent on mind health, as a peaceful mind enlivens
a joyful spirit. The I Ching inspired development of
practices like chi gong, tai chi and meditation as ways to
cultivate a calm and peaceful mind. People often notice
that when they practice tai chi or chi gong, they become
calmer and more effective in their current tasks.
Meditation is another effective way to improve mind
health as it helps you let go of stale and stuck emotions
and allows your mind to become calm and aware.
These practices nurture your intuition and develop your
spiritual awareness, which gently guides your actions
and brings greater peace to our life.

Freedom From
Emotional Entanglement

Emotions are a natural part of life that communicate and express your inner world. Understanding your emotions can help you to improve and grow, but unhealthy emotions can also block you from seeing the truth. You may be a genius when it comes to helping others solve their emotional problems and yet paralyzed by your own. This is because you can be a detached and objective observer when you analyze other peoples' issues, but often lose the objectivity when you are in the midst of experiencing your own upheaval and turmoil. Healthy emotion comes from healing past traumas as well as full acceptance of yourself and others. It provides the vehicle for self-discovery, deeper connection with others and a richer life experience.

Cultivate a Balanced Personality
by Balancing Your Five Elements

Your personality mirrors your core Element. Wood is Authoritative, Heart is Passionate, Earth is Caring, Metal is Methodical and Water is Wise. Your inherent talent supports and builds your confidence and helps you to meet your challenges. The key to a healthy personality is to understand your core personality, strengths and weakness, and to work on overcoming your challenges so that you are balanced. Challenges are like rocks— they can either be a stepping-stone or a stumbling block. The ultimate objective is to cultivate the positive attributes of all Five Elements for a balanced personality. The joy in life is a dance between accepting your gifts and exploring new ones.

Develop Your Intuition
and Creativity

Intuition and creativity are your higher mind, which come from nurturing your subconscious and trusting its expressions. Intellectual learning helps you acquire knowledge, and yet a busy mind filled with excessive knowledge can inhibit the development of intuition and block your access to creativity. Incessant mental distractions, survival worries and ruminations, and negative emotions all act like a cloudy sky separating you from the North Star. It's easy to see why many people lose their way and never reach their potential. The most effective way to clear these patterns is to nurture self-awareness and the reflective mind. Use contemplation, invocation and meditation to awaken the power inherent within you to help guide and manifest your life.

Wood Element
Mental Health

Energetic imbalance as a Wood Element can lead to anger, resentment, frustration and depression. These feelings, when unchecked, can become a torrential storm overwhelming the recipient of your emotional outburst. Careless diet, prolonged stress, recreational drugs and alcohol can also weaken liver energy and create a brittle nervous system.

Solutions:

Exercise. Go for a walk, jog, bike, swim or dance to activate flow of your energy and drain off your anger and aggression.

Undertake a cleansing detoxification program to support the balance of your liver energy network.

Express your feelings through words instead of a temper tantrum. Use words such as, "I am uncomfortable or unhappy or angry or upset" to describe your feelings instead of unleashing them like a destructive downpour.

Keep a journal to record your feelings and then burn it in a ritual.

Invocation for Wood Element

Invocations are prayers or mantra that are sincere request for help and intervention from the divine realm. Recite or chant the following invocation 36 times daily:

Divine One of Peace and Tranquility,
Please help me release my anger,
Resentment and frustrations.
I am forever grateful.
Thank you.

Acu-Release Technique™
for Trauma and Blockage Release (ART)

Emotional and physical traumas can come from abuse, relationship breakup, accidents and losses that can lead to energy blockage and result in physical or emotional imbalance, such as illness, pain, emotional disorder, unfulfilling relationship, financial problem and low energy. Acu-Release Technique (ART) is an energy healing modality from Infinichi Coaching that has successfully helped many people release blockages that prevented them from achieving their life's potential. ART will help you resolve past emotional traumas that have become stumbling blocks that have adversely affected your Elemental health and therefore your happiness.

ART
for the Wood Element

1. Establish intention by verbalizing the following:
   - o I have (blockages) _____ that prevent me from finding joy, peace, health, prosperity and fulfillment in my life.
   - o I want to release these blockages so that I can be free from suffering and unhappiness.
   - o I have the power to change and heal in order to experience joy, peace, health, prosperity and fulfillment in my life.

2. Press and hold Acupoint Liver 3 (see Appendix) and verbalize the following:
   - o The (emotional trauma) _____ has affected me in my health, my mind, my relationship and my life.
   - o I now forever release this trauma from my being and my life.

3. Give permission to let go by verbalizing the following:
   - o Thank you for giving me the strength to get my (feeling) _____out so now I can release the blockage and heal.
   - o I am grateful to be empowered by the divine to actualize my life.

4. You can now stop pressing and let go of holding the acupoint.

Fire Element
Mental Health

As a Fire Elemental type, you are able to express feelings passionately, yet you can be vulnerable to criticism and your feelings easily hurt. You may also possess a strong ego, and you have a difficult time getting along with others, which ultimately leads to isolation and loneliness. Because of your need for acknowledgement and validation, you can easily become co-dependent. You need to learn how to be vulnerable without giving up emotional independence.

Solutions:

Your need for recognition can be fulfilled, first, by accepting yourself.

Each morning, think of one positive attribute or trait you like about yourself and feel gratefulness.

Step back and learn to be objective and analytical in order to make decisions that are not colored by your emotions

Practice Fire Element Chi Gong to strengthen your heart energy network (see Appendix).

The antidote for hurt and sadness is laughter. Watch your favorite comedy show, read a funny book and talk to a friend who always makes you laugh.

Invocation for Fire Element

Invocations are prayers or mantra that are sincere request for help and intervention from the divine realm. Recite or chant the following invocation 36 times daily:

Dear Divine One of Joy,
Please help me release the pain and hurt
And help me let go of my negative attachments.
I am forever grateful.
Thank you.

ART ™
for the Fire Element

1. Establish intention by verbalizing the following:
   o I have (blockages) _____ that prevent me from finding joy, peace, health, prosperity and fulfillment in my life.
   o I want to release these blockages so that I can be free from suffering and unhappiness.
   o I have the power to change and heal in order to experience joy, peace, health, prosperity and fulfillment.

2. Press and hold Acupoint Heart 7 (see Appendix) and verbalize the following:
   o The (emotional trauma) _____ has affected me in my health, my mind, my relationship and my life.
   o I now forever release this trauma from my being and my life.

3. Give permission to let go by verbalizing the following:
   o Thank you for giving me the strength to get my
     (feeling) _____out so now I can release the
     blockage and heal.
   o I am grateful to be empowered by the divine to
     actualize my life.

4. You can now stop pressing and let go of holding the
   acupoint.

Earth Element
Mental Health

In Chinese medicine, Earth energy is responsible for information processing and thinking. When you are worried, over-thinking, obsessing combined with a poor diet, you can become out of balance, leading to brain fog and fixation. Earth Element oversees nourishment, not only for your body but also for your spirit. When your Earth Element is in balance, you are happy, healthy, loving and giving.

Solutions:

Walk barefoot in the outdoors; dig in your toes and feel your connection to the earth.

Evaluate your thinking. Is it clear or muddled? If muddled, take a moment and breathe in fresh air deeply for a few minutes. How is your mind now?

Who do you support; who supports you? Get your support system together.

Set aside a specific time daily to ruminate and write down your worries and concerns. For example, devote 30 minutes from 12-12:30 p.m. daily to rumination. Then accept it and move on.

Drink tea containing chamomile, valerian, jujube or take the herbal formula Calm-Fort to relax your mind.

Invocation for Earth Element

Invocations are prayers or mantra that are sincere request for help and intervention from the divine realm. Recite or chant the following invocation 36 times daily:

> *Dear Divine One of Constancy,*
> *Please help me release all my worries and anxiety*
> *And strengthen my foundation.*
> *I am forever grateful.*
> *Thank you.*

ART™
for Earth Element

1. Establish intention by verbalizing the following:
   - o I have (blockages) _____ that prevent me from finding joy, peace, health, prosperity and fulfillment in my life.
   - o I want to release these blockages so that I can be free from suffering and unhappiness.
   - o I have the power to change and heal in order to experience joy, peace, health, prosperity and fulfillment in my life.

2. Press and hold Acupoint Spleen 3 (see Appendix) and verbalize the following:
   - o The (emotional trauma) _____ has affected me in my health, my mind, my relationship and my life.
   - o I now forever release this trauma from my being and my life.

3. Give permission to let go by verbalizing the following:
   o Thank you for giving me the strength to get my (feeling) _____ out so now I can release the blockage and heal.
   o I am grateful to be empowered by the divine to actualize my life.

4. You can now stop pressing and let go of the acupoint.

Metal Element
Mental Health

If you are an unbalanced, opinionated and inflexible Metal person, it is quite possible that you subscribe to long-held principles and beliefs and that as a perfectionist, you can be very critical, both of yourself and of others. Cultivating tolerance and acceptance of your own attributes and those of others is a very important aspect of bringing your element into balance. Whether you perceive these attributes to be positive or negative, your acceptance of them will stop critical thinking and help you to embrace change.

Solutions:

Toyota refined the practice of Kaizen, or continuous improvement, which is based on incremental and not radical changes. This practice vaulted the company into the top ranks in the world. Stop expecting perfection. Instead, keep a list of small changes you can make regularly and be happy with it.

Practice Metal Element Chi Gong to support healthy lung energy network (See Appendix).

Invocation for Metal Element

Invocations are prayers or mantra that are sincere request for help and intervention from the divine realm. Recite or chant the following invocation 36 times daily:

Dear Divine One of Great Compassion,
Please help me release all my sadness,
And allow me to gain profound understanding
Of the human condition.
I am forever grateful.
Thank you!

ART™
for the Metal Element

1. Establish intention by verbalizing the following:
   o I have (blockages) _____ that prevent me from finding joy, peace, health, prosperity and fulfillment in my life.
   o I want to release these blockages so that I can be free from suffering and unhappiness.
   o I have the power to change and heal in order to experience joy, peace, health, prosperity and fulfillment in my life.

2. Press and hold Acupoint Lung 9 (see Appendix) and verbalize the following:
   o The (emotional trauma) _____ has affected me in my health, my mind, my relationship and my life.
   o I now forever release this trauma from my being and my life.

3. Give permission to let go by verbalizing the following:

   o Thank you for giving me the strength to get my (feeling) _____ out so now I can release the blockage and heal.

   o I am grateful to be empowered by the divine to actualize my life.

4. You can now stop pressing and let go of the acupoint.

Water Element
Mental Health

It is natural for your Water energy to have two sides: one side is vulnerable and the other fearless. When you are tired, and your energy is out of balance, you may feel cautious and unwilling to take risks even though you are very creative and capable. It is also possible for you to become anxious when you are in situations you cannot control, like flying in an airplane. The solution is for you to learn the facts and then apply your wisdom to any problems that occur.

Solutions:

Starting tonight, put paper and a pen on your bedside table, and begin keeping a dream journal.

Your dreams can lead and inspire you and also clue you into your concerns, so that you can address your fear and move forward.

Practice Water Element Chi Gong to reinforce your endurance and will (See Appendix).

Take Water Element herbal supplement to support your fearless kidney-adrenal energy (See Resources).

Invocation for Water Element

Invocations are prayers or mantra that are sincere request for help and intervention from the divine realm. Recite or chant the following invocation 36 times daily:

Dear Divine One of Great Courage,
Please help me release all my fears
And help me strengthen my will.
I am forever grateful.
Thank you!

ART ™
for the Water Element

1. Establish intention by verbalizing the following:
   o I have (blockages) _____ that prevent me from finding joy, peace, health, prosperity and fulfillment in my life.
   o I want to release these blockages so that I can be free from suffering and unhappiness.
   o I have the power to change and heal in order to experience joy, peace, health, prosperity and fulfillment in my life.

2. Press and hold Acupoint Kidney 3 (see Appendix) and verbalize the following:
   o The (emotional trauma) _____ has affected me in my health, my mind, my relationship and my life.
   o I now forever release this trauma from my being and my life.

3. Give permission to let go by verbalizing the following:
   o Thank you for giving me the strength to get my
     (feeling) _____out so now I can release the
     blockage and heal.
   o I am grateful to be empowered by the divine to
     actualize my life.

4. You can now stop pressing and let go of the acupoint.

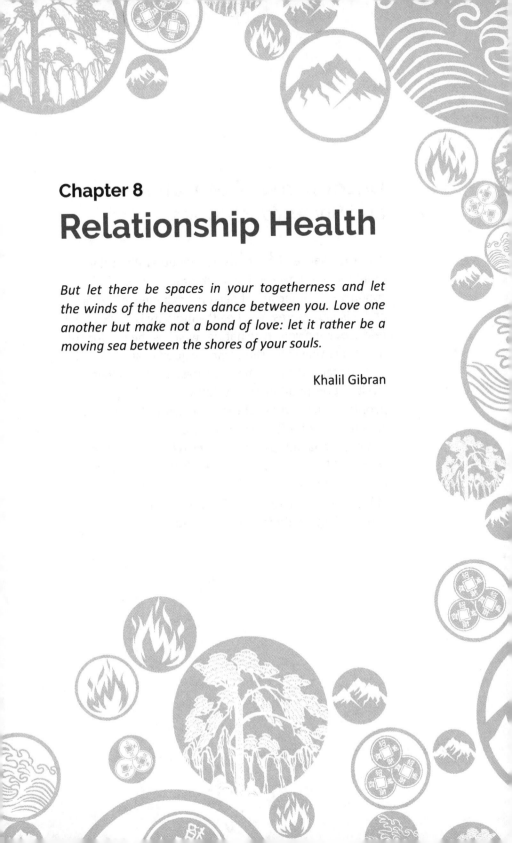

Chapter 8
Relationship Health

But let there be spaces in your togetherness and let the winds of the heavens dance between you. Love one another but make not a bond of love: let it rather be a moving sea between the shores of your souls.

Khalil Gibran

Uncover Your True Nature
and Show Your Virtues

Your experience of relationships, whether it's social or intimate, is governed by your internal rules of conduct—a composite of personal experience, social and religious mores. Yet, healthy morality is really about re-discovering your true nature, which is the product of the Divine Universe. The common good in all mankind is characterized by five basic virtues: loving kindness, civility, appropriateness, faithfulness and wisdom. Yet people often fall short of these virtues in their conduct. Your behavior is often a reaction from your mental and emotional temperament, which corresponds to your core Element. When you work on restoring your Elemental balance, you can recover your innate quality of being naturally virtuous. The result is more satisfying and fulfilling relationships in your life.

Guided by
Your Conscience

Moral health is central in any spiritual work and is the foundation to gratifying relationships. Years of meditation, spiritual practices or prayers can be fruitless unless all five virtues are restored. You do not have to struggle or search widely for spiritual achievement. Everything you need is within your original healthy nature. Be guided by your conscience, and remember that you have your own path to self-discovery. Continuous observation of your own behavior and self-acceptance and improvement can eventually resolve the obstructions to being naturally virtuous.

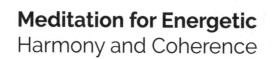

Meditation for Energetic
Harmony and Coherence

According to Chinese medicine, when the energy within
an organ network is excessive, blocked or insufficient, it
causes emotional imbalance. This will not only impact
the health of your mind, but also may damage your
relationships. Ancient master physicians designed
harmonizing meditations to balance the energy swings
of each of the five Elements. In the following pages, you
will learn how these meditations can help round the
edges of the forceful, authoritative Wood personality,
bring consistency to the passionate energies of the
Fire Element, advocate self-care to the nurturing Earth
personality, loosen the strictness and rigidity of the
Metal personality, and open up the mysterious Water
personality.

Part of a fulfilling and meaningful life comes from
achieving harmony and energetic coherence with your
loved ones, friends, neighbors, co-workers and people
in the world, in general. This is also the foundation of
peace on our beautiful planet. Let's begin this adventure
inwards, to the realm where the physical and the
spiritual intertwine.

Wood Element
Appropriateness

Being appropriate can be described as being just right or suitable in any given situation. However, this can be quite challenging as there are no absolute rules in life. Tricky, right? An action suitable in one situation may not be in another. That's just common sense. So how does one navigate appropriateness in all situations? Let's look to ancient teachings. The Element associated with appropriateness is Wood, and its moral correspondence is integrity. We often identify moral issues as good or bad, right or wrong, grace or sin. This dualistic approach can hinder our growth and spiritual maturity.

Moralizing alienates people, and judgment often results in defensiveness, rather than reflection—definitely NOT what you intended to inspire. The path to moral health lies in being truthful, natural and appropriate in every situation. This takes spiritual progress and adherence to the Golden Rule—"do unto others as you would have them do unto you." Yep. That little nugget has existed for eons, and still works best.

Wood Element
Compatibilities

As a Wood person, you tend to have a strong personality that some may identify as Type A, inflexible, overbearing, or competitive. Attributes that help you succeed in completing projects and goals at work may backfire in your personal relationships. This, inevitably, leads to stress and tension with your loved ones.

You may have an easier time with Water people, who are likely to go along with your flow, Fire people, who also share your passion, and Earth people, who are accommodating and supportive. The propensity of being overbearing and stubborn may create resistance and rebellion, if your loved ones perceive your aggressiveness as being directed at them.

You will most certainly clash with Metal people, who do not change easily or respond well to new ideas that are abruptly imposed on them. Even at work, you may lose employees or co-workers if you are too intense all the time, making people uncomfortable. You may also easily and unwittingly hurt the feelings of Fire personalities.

To begin: Channel your abundant positive energy to motivate, cheerlead and inspire. People will follow you if they feel like you've listened, acknowledged their perspectives, and compromised. Then, and only then, can you proceed and push forward with extraordinary creativity and remarkable energy.

Wood Element
in Love

Wood Element love begins during childhood, when children experience the natural love between themselves and their parents. This is called the virtue of Xiao—or filial piety—a love that grows and expands as the child ages to include love for siblings, then relatives, then friends, their country, and ultimately, love for humanity. This natural human virtue explains why you, as a Wood person, aspire to give and receive sweet love, and want to feel cherished, respected and understood by a partner who acknowledges and honors your feelings.

In intimate exchange, you cannot be rushed; you often need time and space for gentle touch, slow, sensual exploration and prolonged love-making. It must be noted that you cannot change gears quickly, and you may find forceful love play to be very off-putting. When you feel treasured and safe within a warm relationship, you as a Wood lover are able to reveal your intuitive, loving abilities that even you cannot completely understand—but then, we know that Wood has a natural ability to love and be loved.

Energy Harmonizing Meditation
for the Wood Element

Begin by sitting comfortably in a chair with your spine straight, not leaning against the seatback. Curl your tongue so that the bottom is pressed against the roof of your mouth. Pull your chin inward to straighten your neck. Breathe from your abdomen, deeply, slowly and smoothly. Focus your mind with a relaxed intent.

You will be guiding the energies with your hands throughout your body. The right hand is the energy "projection" hand. Place it over your Wood Element, represented by the liver, under your ribs, on the right abdomen, against the skin. The left hand is the energy "receiver" hand. Place it about six inches from your heart, not touching the skin.

Visualize the corresponding color energy, in this case green energy, entering from your right projector hand into your liver and gallbladder. Transmit this energy through your body to your heart, where the green energy transforms into red energy, and is received by your left receiver hand. Do this for 10-15 minutes at least once a day. You will notice the more you practice, the more you will feel at ease with those you have previously come into conflict.

The reason why the harmonizing meditation ends in your heart is because love is the manifestation of the Fire Element and the heart energy network. Love is the uniting and forgiving force of any separation and/or transgression, and fills your being with gratitude and happiness.

Fire Element
Loving Kindness

Loving kindness is the core of a healthy personality, and the heart of universal nature, which sustains all life. It includes being protective, nurturing and loving. Its element is Fire, and its moral correspondence is benevolence. However, even loving kindness has a negative aspect when it's taken to the extreme. When you spoil someone with excessive benevolence, in Buddhism, it is called "idiot compassion". You are actually harming them and causing problems for your relationship, and their relationship with the world. For example: Mother Nature provides just enough sustenance, and she does not over indulge. It is man whose greed drives him to want more. That is at the root of most conflicts. Balance dictates that once you have enough, you can help those less fortunate; but give just enough assistance so that they can stand on their own.

Fire Element
Compatibilities

As a Fire Elemental type, you are able to feel deeply and express feelings that move others. However, you are also very vulnerable to criticism, and your feelings can be easily hurt because you want people to like, love and adore you. Therefore, when someone expresses any displeasure directed towards you, your ego may be crushed. Your hurt may lead you to withdraw into isolation, loneliness and depression. You will most likely have more challenges with the critical Metal and elusive Water personalities.

Innately, however, you are an optimistic, sunny and cheerful person. Due to your emotional sensitivity, you need to surround yourself with positive, supportive and loving people, like the nurturing Earth type. You share commonality with the passionate nature of Wood, but need to learn how to deal with criticism. This may help you to grow, change and improve, which is never bad, spiritually, speaking. When you are able to receive people's feedback as an act of care and affection as opposed to an offense, you will transform your insecurity into courage.

Fire Element
in Love

If your Fire energy is true to form, then you are flirtatious and enjoy calling attention to yourself. You love fantasy, being naked, having the lights on, and unpredictable moves. You probably want to talk and want your partner to talk back to you. Wild talk, animal sounds—it's all part of the fun for your high-octane Fire energy. Immediately after lovemaking, you are apt to go on to the next thing; checking text messages for example. This behavior is not intended to be dismissive to your partner. It is simply your nature. However, be aware that this can be perceived as unloving or just plain rude. You may have to make some compromises in order to be in a relationship with a lover who is one of the other four elements, but it will be well worth the effort for both of you.

Energy Harmonizing Meditation
for the Fire Element

Begin by sitting comfortably in a chair with your spine straight, not leaning against the seatback. Curl your tongue so that the bottom of your tongue is pressed against the roof of your mouth. Pull your chin inward to straighten your neck. Breathe from your abdomen, deeply, slowly and smoothly. Focus your mind with relaxed intent.

You will be guiding the energies with your hands. The right hand is the energy "projection" hand. Place it over your Fire Element, represented by the heart, against the skin. The left hand is the energy "receiver" hand; place it about six inches from your heart, not touching the skin.

Visualize the corresponding color energy, in this case red energy, entering from your right projector hand into your heart. Transmit this energy back out from your heart, where the red energy remains red, and is received by your left receiver hand. Do this for 10–15 minutes, at least once a day. You will notice, the more you practice, the more you will feel at ease with those you have previously come into conflict.

The reason that the harmonizing meditation ends in your heart, is because love is the manifestation of the Fire Element, and the heart energy network. Love is the uniting, forgiving force of any separation and/or transgression, and fills your being with gratitude and happiness.

Earth Element
Faithfulness

Pure faithfulness comes from personal growth and spiritual maturity. A heart full of pure faithfulness brings a beautiful response from the universe.
The element of faithfulness is Earth and its moral correspondence is being trustworthy. When taken to the extreme, faithfulness sometimes begets discrimination and exclusion, which contributes to separation rather than integration. Natural faithfulness comes from the trust that the sun will always rise up each day and be there for our benefit, though obscured by the cloud.

Earth Element
Compatibility

As an Earth person, you are prone to being giving, thoughtful and generous—sometimes, to a fault. You have a tendency to overcompensate, and make up for what is lacking in others, so you can easily give more than you receive and your interpersonal relationships become off balance. You tend to also worry too much for your own good. The image of an airplane cabin comes to mind. As the preparation for take off occurs, you are informed that if the cabin should ever lose pressure, an oxygen mask will drop from the ceiling. You are further instructed to put the mask on yourself first before helping and tending to the person next to you. This is the principle for you to follow in your own life. Seek to nurture yourself while tending to others.

Interestingly, your Earth Element is compatible with all the other Elements as you are the mediator, peace-maker and diplomat. However, form healthy boundaries so that people cannot just barge into your life, without regard to your personal space or energy. In the worst of circumstances, they may use you as a doormat. Let people know where that boundary is, diplomatically and firmly. You will be glad you did.

Earth Element
in Love

You have a tendency to be easy-going and are able to
have a wonderful relationship with any of the other
Elemental types. You are welcoming and have a good
sense of humor. Most Earth people love to eat, sleep
and loll in bed ... does that sound like you? Your Element
is the one that most enjoys the familiar, earthy smell
of bodies. You also relish gentle, smooth caressing and
may have noticed that your belly, chest, underarms
and throat are particularly sensitive to touch. As an
Earth person, you probably don't have a neat and tidy
bedroom, and you don't want to go over-the-top with
scary lovemaking practices. You may crack a joke and
laugh at yourself or your partner ... you are truly a
natural lover.

Energy Harmonizing Meditation
for the Earth Element

Begin by sitting comfortably in a chair with your spine straight, not leaning against the seatback. Curl your tongue so that the bottom of your tongue is pressed against the roof of your mouth. Pull your chin inward to straighten your neck. Breathe from your abdomen, deeply, slowly and smoothly. Focus your mind with relaxed intent.

You will be guiding the energies with your hands. The right hand is the energy "projection" hand. Place it over your Earth Element, represented by the spleen and stomach in center of your upper abdomen, against the skin. The left hand is the energy "receiver" hand. Place it about six inches from your heart, not touching the skin.

Visualize the corresponding color energy, in this case yellow energy, entering from your right projector hand into your stomach, spleen and pancreas. Transmit this energy through your body to your heart, where the yellow energy transforms into red energy, and is received by your left receiver hand. Do this for 10-15 minutes at least once a day. The more you practice, the more you will feel at ease.

The reason that the harmonizing meditation ends in your heart, is because love is the manifestation of the Fire Element and the heart energy network. Love is the uniting and forgiving force of any separation and/or transgression, and fills your being with gratitude and happiness.

Metal Element
Orderliness or Civility

Orderliness or civility brings simplicity and unity to the spirit, and manifests at the emotional, physical, financial and social levels of life. At the personal relationship level, it is the well-organized life. Its element is Metal and its moral correspondence is humility. You should always seek balance in exercising your virtue with people, because extreme formality or decorum can sometimes beget disorder or rebellion in those less inclined to those traits. Listen with respect and humility and allow flexibility when necessary to facilitate peace.

Metal Element
Compatibility

As a Metal Element person, if you are imbalanced, you may become opinionated, rigid and inflexible. You may find yourself clashing with Wood Element's brashness, and Fire's sponteneity. You will find compatiblity with the easygoing natures of Earth and Water people. Your elegance and refined manners easily attract people to you. They may, however, also be intimated by your aloof, cold and detached moods. Beware the hubris of thinking, "This is the way I am. If people don't like it, then lump it, and move on." Everyone you meet is a work-in-progress—including yourself—and perfectionism can become an obstacle to your wish of attaining closeness in your relationships. So loosen up and cut people and yourself some slack. Be spontaneous. Put down the scheduling app, and let go of your planning a little. You'll never know what adventures lie ahead.

Metal Element
in Love

Every Metal lover is different, but in general, you may think that you already know everything there is to know about love-making. You probably enjoy preparing and planning for action ahead of time, figuring it all out step by step, like a party planner. (Remember that scheduler app?) Then, during love-making, your mind may wander outside of yourself, as you check on how you are doing. Since you are interested in performance, you tend to like mirrors so you can observe your moves and your body. Try to remember that making love really is about the two of you being present together, and in the most loving of circumstances, about pleasing the other person. Try to let go of critical self-evaluation, and enjoy the ride, so to speak.

Although you are not naturally an empathetic or intuitive lover, you do your best to perform well and please your partner. Even though you tend to keep your emotions hidden, you appreciate acknowledgement of your prowess as a lover, so be certain to ask your partner to provide that for you.

Energy Harmonizing Meditation
for the Metal Element

Begin by sitting comfortably in a chair with your spine straight, not leaning against the seatback. Curl your tongue so that the bottom of your tongue is pressed against the roof of your mouth. Pull your chin inward to straighten your neck. Breathe from your abdomen, deeply, slowly and smoothly. Focus your mind with relaxed intent.

You will be guiding the energies with your hands. The right hand is the energy "projection" hand. Place it over your Metal Element, represented by the right lung, on the right side of your chest, against the skin. The left hand is the energy "receiver" hand. Place it about six inches from your heart, not touching the skin.

Visualize the corresponding color energy, in this case white energy, entering from your right projector hand into your lungs. Transmit this energy through your body to your heart, where the white energy transforms into red energy, and is received by your left receiver hand. Do this for 10-15 minutes at least once a day. The more you practice, the more you will feel at ease.

The reason why the harmonizing meditation ends in your heart is because love is the manifestation of the Fire Element and the heart energy network. Love is the uniting and forgiving force of any separation and transgressions and fills your being with gratitude and happiness.

Water Element
Wisdom

The wisdom of a sage cannot be obtained by reading, learning or thinking about the subject. Those processes may give us a high intellectual vision, but do not make us act wisely, or enter us into the realm of spirit. There are three levels of wisdom. The first comes from our own life experience. The second is the unspeakable, silent wisdom from within, and is associated with the balanced mind that always responds appropriately. The third level, only attainable through spiritual cultivation, is indescribable and comes from the pure spirit. The Element of wisdom is Water and its moral correspondence is discernment. True wisdom is to learn from, and accept, each life situation as part of our growth.

Water Element
Compatibilities

As a Water Element person you may be naturally cautious, especially if you were raised by nervous parents, or have encountered pain or failure in relationships and life events. It is also possible for you to become anxious when you are in situations filled with unknowns, such as being in a new relationship. Your tendency to hold back that which is in your heart and mind may cause distrust and frustration on the other person's part. You are less interested in Fire personalities, but find solace with Earth types. You have an appreciation of the guiding nature of Wood people. Your path to peace and contentment is for you to learn the facts about an individual and his or her intentions. Ask for their patience, and then at the appropriate time and place, apply courage and wisdom to reveal your inner feelings and thoughts. In other words, when you trust them, get off the fence and go for it! Understand that this is all part of the journey. The more you practice being open and honest, the easier it gets. Using the Energy Harmonizing Meditation will greatly reduce your fears and allow a deeper connection to others to take hold.

Water Element
in Love

As a mysterious, invisible Water lover, you are very different from the romantic Wood, flirtatious Fire, easy-going Earth, or goal-oriented Metal. You are a quiet lover, who may never make a sound. Your energy is filled with deeply addictive, seductive pleasures waiting to be expressed. Although water is cold and hidden, it is also fluid and soft; an all-powerful, forward-moving tidal wave that swells and surges! It is the instinctual life-giving power of creation. Not a bad way to describe yourself, in bed!

You probably appreciate darkness and privacy in order to feel completely safe and free to display your creative passion. You may prefer to have doors locked, curtains drawn and blinds shut; you also may like being covered in pillows or a fluffy blanket. You are instinctive, and your energy wants to go deeper and deeper; filling every hollow and yielding to every protrusion. Once uncovered, your level of physical giving and receiving is intense and passionate.

Energy Harmonizing Meditation
for the Water Element

Begin by sitting comfortably in a chair with your spine straight, not leaning against the seatback. Curl your tongue so that the bottom of your tongue is pressed against the roof of your mouth. Pull your chin inward to straighten your neck. Breath from your abdomen, deeply, slowly and smoothly. Focus your mind with relaxed intent.

You will be guiding the energies with your hands. The right hand is the energy "projection" hand. Place it over your Water Element, represented by the right kidneys in your lower back, against the skin. The left hand is the energy "receiver" hand. Place it about six inches from your heart, not touching the skin.

Visualize the corresponding color energy, in this case blue energy, entering from your right projector hand, into your kidneys and adrenals. Transmit this energy through your abdominal cavity to your heart, where the blue energy transforms into red energy, and is received by your left receiver hand. Do this for 10-15 minutes at least once a day. The more you practice, the more you will feel at ease.

The reason why the harmonizing meditation ends in your heart is because love is the manifestation of the Fire Element and the heart energy network. Love is the uniting and forgiving force of any separation and/or transgression, and fills your being with gratitude and happiness.

Chapter 9

Financial Health

*We should manage our fortunes as we do our health—
enjoy it when good, be patient when it is bad, and never
apply violent remedies except in an extreme necessity.*

Francois de La Rochefoucauld

Financial Health is About
Sustaining Others
as Well as Yourself

Finances are an important part of being a healthy person. However, there is some misinterpretation and misunderstanding that occurs when we discuss wealth. For example: Our human bodies are actually a part of our wealth. When we treasure and take care of our bodies, we are also taking care of our wealth. Having financial wellness also means being responsible stewards of our planet, as we draw sustenance from it. Whatever form our wealth might take, it is our job is to treasure, cultivate and preserve our gifts, so we can use those gifts to sustain others, as well as ourselves.

Financial Independence
and Self Sufficiency

Financial health is about cultivating independence and self-sufficiency. Every person has opportunities to achieve financial health in his or her life. Contrary to what some may think, your financial health is not dependent on your birth, education, inheritance, job, the stock market or winning the lottery. We've all heard the stories, and seen people on various TV shows who have had extraordinary opportunities, degrees from Ivy League schools, inherited fortunes, and won lotteries but still ended up financially destitute. I'm sure you've asked yourself, "What went wrong?" Conversely, we've admired those from appallingly difficult circumstances, who've had many challenges to overcome, who became moguls and masters—Oprah Winfrey comes to mind. The key to financial wellness is to first cultivate the correct attitude towards financial matters, and then craft a plan specific to your unique talents, goals and objectives. You then need the discipline to follow and execute the plan consistently.

Correct Financial
Attitude

In order to achieve financial health, you must have the
right attitude. Judeo-Christian teachings in the West,
and Buddhism in the East, have led most people to
believe that money is the root of evil, that it corrupts
one's character, breaks families apart and breeds wars.
Certainly history is full of countless examples of these
failings, and our personal experiences confirm the perils
of money, as well. No question, that if not managed
correctly, all energies, in excess can become out of
control and destructive.

So. What is the "correct financial attitude?" You must
accept that managing your finances is a part of living a
responsible life. You also need to realize that creating
financial health is important to sustaining your life's
purpose. Money is just another form of energy, or
chi, which allows you the freedom and ability to make
choices and decisions for your life, including those for
your family and your community. What you choose for
your career, how you blend your passion and talent
in alignment with your mission, and how you express
your creativity is all part of your journey. Once you
understand this vantage point, you can view your
finances objectively, rather than seeing them as good or
bad, moral or immoral.

Your Element Determines
Your Approach to Financial Health

Your Element possesses traits that predispose you to unique tendencies and styles of financial handling. For example, the Wood person tends to spend impulsively and make gambles, the Water personality is prone to being risk averse, potentially missing out on good opportunities, the Earth Element is generous to a fault, the Metal person is inclined to have expensive tastes and the Fire personality tends to spend to feel good. Understanding your Elemental personality disposition can help you work on a new and improved approach to enrich your financial health.

Money is an Expression
of Your Productive Energy

Money is neutral—it's neither good or bad, it is simply an expression of your productive energy and depending on how you manage it, it can be positive or negative. Say a farmer uses his energy to grow rice. He then takes the rice and exchanges it for eggs from the chicken farmer, clothes from the tailor and farm tools from the metal smith. For all the parties involved in the trade, the expression of each of their productive energies became money. Money is portable and provides freedom to exchange goods and services without the need to lug rice everywhere you go!

Money is a valuation tool that determines what the worth of your productive energy is. If you are able to provide highly sought after goods and services then your energy expression commands a high valuation. The important thing about money is to recognize that it is the energy we use to sustain us, materially, and allow us the freedom to live out our lives in a constructive, and meaningful way, as well as to help others in need.

Three Types
of Monetary Energy Corruption

Teenagers are good examples of how energy can go awry. Their excess energy often drives them to behaviors that can be destructive to themselves and others. This can include wild parties, loud music, smoking, drinking and taking drugs, indiscriminate sexual behaviors and violence. These expressions of out of control energy lead to unfortunate and sometimes fatal consequences, such as drug overdoses, driving under the influence and sometimes, tragically, death.

Money energy is no different. When this energy is out of control through greed or reckless spending, the consequences are dire for the person, and for those who rely on them as well.

The Difference Between
the Miser and the Frugal

The first type of financial corruption is a wealthy but miserly person, who ruthlessly takes from others, and hordes his or her wealth, but is loath to share or use it to benefit their own family, community or society. This person is often miserable, and the negative deeds lead to bad consequences within that family. However, being frugal on the other hand is a virtue. It is the daily acts of reducing waste and conserving resources in order so that you can share with more people.

Don't Get Tripped Up
by Greed

The second type of energy corruption is driven by greed and the insatiable appetite to accumulate evermore. This impacts many people in severe and dire ways. This person cannot help but perpetuate behaviors that may be illegal and criminal due to greed. Bernie Madoff personified this type of greedy individual. In a span of 20–30 years, he swindled investors with his infamous Ponzi scheme, bilking billions from foundations, retirement plans and individuals and leaving thousands of people adversely scarred.

Watch Out for Enslavement
by Money

The third type of monetary energy corruption comes from enslavement by money. This type of person accumulates wealth, and buys many things with it, only to come under the pressure to maintain their things and lifestyle. They no longer are free, but rather enslaved by money—they are addicted to external trappings, and how those are viewed by society. A personal friend of mine who worked very hard and earned a lot of money, bought a ten million dollar house. He had a large mortgage on it. When every one of his businesses experienced a downturn during the recession, he developed panic disorders. His every waking hour was involved in how to maintain his lifestyle. Unfortunately, he died at his desk, from a massive heart attack, at age 42. He exchanged his life force for money.

Financial Energy
Transformation

Learn the alchemy of financial energy transformation, and how to cultivate, and manage, the manifested energy of money. Financial energy cultivation is no different than human energy cultivation. It involves the process of sourcing, gathering, growing, cultivating, deploying and regenerating energy that started out raw, like physical labor, or intellectual development, and transforming it along the way, refining and channeling it purposefully, and finally sublimating it to a higher form of spiritual energy. The alchemy of financial energy transformation is akin to the process of gold production.

The Alchemy of
Gold Making

The method of mining for gold illustrates the process of
energy transformation. Even before the gathering begins,
the entire process starts with preliminary discovery
to identify the source of the mineral ore deposits.
Once the source is determined the gathering can then
begin. Mounds of dirt are taken from the ground and
transported to the refinery. There the dirt is sifted, sorted
and filtered to allow the mineral metals to be extracted.
Next they are fed into a furnace to separate out the
other metals and minerals so that gold can be refined to
a higher concentration. Over time more gold is refined
to various percentages of purity. It is then accumulated
in quantities required for use in manufacturing, jewelry
making and coin minting—transformations that
increased its original value. As the products are sold or
traded its value rises, which makes it exchangeable for
other valuables or services that serve your purpose.

You Don't Have to Have
a High Paying Job to Accumulate Abundant Wealth

Margaret Southern was a humble, special-needs teacher in Greenville, South Carolina. When she died in 2012 at the age of 94 she left $8.4 million to her favorite charity, the Community Foundation of Greenville. There are many people like her who did not have high paying jobs but learned to live below their means, saved and invested wisely and overtime accumulated unimaginable wealth that they directed to benefit others less fortunate. She lived a purposeful life, helping children with special needs, and left a legacy that she will be remembered for.

Source of
Financial Energy

Your job or career is by far the biggest source of your financial energy. You exchange your energy or chi for a portable energy in the form of money. In school, you are generally taught that rewards only go to those who are smart and work hard. Later you may come to realize that success and earning abilities in the workplace often come from being likable, creative, or by adding value. The market place puts a premium on these skills, and the top players in any profession get there because of their ability to master them all. With each paycheck the smartest move you can make is to have 10% or more automatically deducted into a separate savings account. Pay your living expenses with the remaining 90% or whatever percentage of your salary you can live on.

Other Overlooked Sources
of Financial Energy

If you have some extra time each week, perhaps you should look for ways to earn extra income around activities or hobbies that you already enjoy doing. For example, a patient of mine—a high school teacher who is passionate about teaching—decided to offer her services to tutor students on weekends. After her first year she realized that her tutoring activities contributed almost 25% extra to her total income. She put all of her earnings from tutoring into her investment account. Another patient, a stay-at-home mom, discovered a line of nutritional products that she personally enjoyed. She decided to join the direct selling company as an independent sales representative. After two years, the income from her very part time work now pays for her family's annual vacation to Europe. Identify activities you enjoy and figure out how you can get paid for doing it. For instance, if you love swimming, how about studying for and getting certified as a lifeguard, which you can do part time.

Taking Financial
Inventory

Everyone needs to do at least some simple budgeting—a financial inventory of where you are each month, how much money is coming in, where and how much is going out, and what's left at the end of the month. It's not unlike a health inventory, because once you know where your deficiencies are, you can take steps to rectify them. Budgeting will give you the power to choose which expenses are not necessary and which are essential. This is critical not only to the survival of a business, but for families as well. Amazingly, a good percentage of people don't have a personal or family budget and don't have a concrete idea where all the money goes. No level of income is ever too high to ignore this counsel. Without a good budget, and the discipline to maintain it, any gains can be undone through overspending. This is the area you have the most ability to control. Yet ironically, it is easier to blame your choice of job, an unlucky investment, high gas prices, or the economy, rather than your spending choices. If you prioritize financial health, you can make an extra effort to save on a consistent and steady basis.

Invest, Grow and Cultivate
Your Financial Energy

Once you've established an automatic savings mechanism, you will need to decide how to invest so that your monetary energy will grow to meet your goals and objectives. Write down two types of goals: long term and short term. Long-term goals may be saving for college tuition for your children. Another goal is retirement. Short-term goals may include buying a condo or a house within the next three years, or saving for orthodontic braces. The time frame of the goals matter because they will help you determine your risk profile when it comes to various investments. Hire a fee-based financial advisor to help you with a financial plan and investment strategy that's tailored to your goals and risk profile. Many online resources also exist for computerized planning advice.

Use Your Capabilities
From the Five Elements

You can assist your financial health in your daily meditation and chi gong practices. Access traits from each of the Five Elements to help you integrate and utilize all your inherent capabilities. In other words, leverage your Elemental strength while cultivating the traits of the other Elements for balanced development of your financial fitness. Consider the Wood Element as your financial growth, and the Fire Element as its expansion. These must be integrated with the Earth Element to help conserve your financial resources, and with the Metal Element to help your resourcefulness with financial matters. Finally, you must integrate the Water Element to regenerate your financial energies.

Financial Advice
for the Wood Element

As a Wood person, it would be wise for you to slow down and cultivate deliberation. Analyze your financial situation and ask yourself whether you are making correct decisions or rash, impulsive ones. You, as a Wood person, need to pay attention to impulsivity, because quick decisions may not serve you well. If your intuition is colored by rebellion, resentment or anger, you can create problems for yourself and those around you. Slow down, do due diligence, take one step at a time, and err on the side of being conservative. You must not sacrifice your principle if you are interested in achieving financial health.

Financial Advice
for the Fire Element

With Fire Elemental types, emotions color reality, so, you will need to control passion, and learn to be objective and analytical in order to make wise financial decisions. Your special ability to connect with and motivate people can easily become the basis for your own financial health. Your passion is your asset, and your exuberant energy can help you manifest material wealth. As a Fire person, it would be especially useful for you to build leadership skills so that you can help others fulfill their goals and dreams.

Financial Advice
for the Earth Element

As an easy-going Earth person, you may have difficulty disciplining yourself and you may have avoided learning effective management of your accumulations in order to create a strong financial foundation. You may also be afraid to hurt other people's feelings, or are reluctant to have others think badly of you. As a result, you unwisely lend or give away your resources, and then your abundant Earth energy loses its balance. You are one of the fortunate ones whose Element naturally engenders abundance. You have an ability to accumulate wealth, and use your wealth to support worthy causes and people you love. People also reciprocate your love and concern, by loving and nurturing you.

Financial Advice
for the Metal Element

Metal people tend to be cautious and conservative. You are probably very good at math and planning for college, retirement, healthcare, etc. The ability to plan ahead can be both an advantage and a disadvantage; planning your finances in advance is a very important life skill. However, when things don't go according to plan, you may become very self-critical.

Your challenge is to learn how to accept and acknowledge yourself as you are. For example, you may think that you are too conservative, or that you failed at a plan that you made, but if you can accept who you are, that will stop the critical self-talk that takes place in your head. In the same vein, you will benefit from cultivating the ability to adapt to new situations. With increased flexibility and self-acceptance, you can begin to let go of the need to be perfect, and to embrace change.

Financial Advice
for the Water Element

As a Water person, it may be more challenging for you to accumulate financial energy because of your overly cautious nature. You are sometimes so cautious that you become stuck, and are afraid to make any move at all. However, while you may not pursue outsized gains you will be content with capital preservation. Moreover, you can educate yourself and find the comfortable point between taking financial risk, and reaping financial reward. With the help of your powerful Water energy, and clear access to your spirit, it is possible for you to manifest your dream of benefitting yourself, your family and friends, your community, and perhaps even the world.

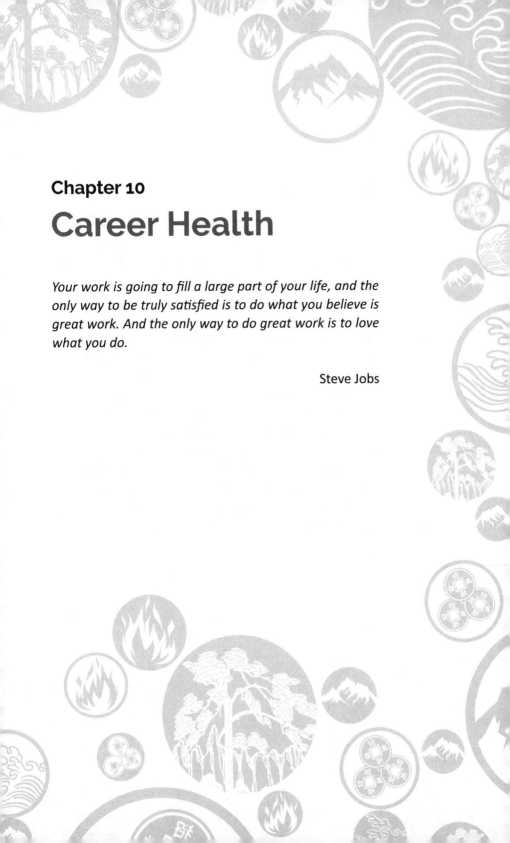

Chapter 10

Career Health

Your work is going to fill a large part of your life, and the only way to be truly satisfied is to do what you believe is great work. And the only way to do great work is to love what you do.

Steve Jobs

Your Career
Is Your Daily Spiritual Expression

Discover where your passion lies, what you are naturally talented in—your gift, and what the marketplace needs are. Determine your answers to the three criteria and align them as one. Imagine fulfilling a marketplace need with something that you are good at and also passionately enjoy doing! Choose wisely, as intentions you put forward shall be answered by the subtle universal response. So if you decide to become successful using malicious business tactics, you may certainly gain money and success, but you will also assuredly hurt people on the way. When you view your career as part of your life purpose and your daily spiritual expression instead of an obligation or enslavement, you will experience meaning and free the creativity from the deep wellspring of your life.

The Secret of Career Bliss
Is Fit Factor

Your Elemental personality expresses traits and characteristics that make you suitable for certain types of work, professions or industries. They make you a natural standout and high performer in certain occupations, leveraging your strengths and innate talents for greater chance of success and fulfillment. Career compatibility describes a job function that makes the most of your natural aptitudes and abilities. For example, when a basketball team is drafting for the team's next guard position and has two equally skilled players to choose from, but one is seven feet tall and the other is six feet in height, then the seven foot person naturally wins out because his height gives him the extra advantage in capturing rebounds and plays around the basket compared to the shorter player. In other words, the position meets the "fit factor" with his natural gifts. Understanding the fit factor can save you from wasted time, effort and resources while trying to find the career meant for you.

The World Judges
a Book by its Cover

In the world we live in, how many people practice the refrain, "Don't judge a book by its cover?" Unfortunately, it's usually the cover of the book that sells! When interacting with people, during a job interview for example, the first impression you give to others can greatly influence how you are treated and viewed in many contexts of everyday life. It's important to note, too, that first impressions tend to be stable and difficult to change. These impressions are based on a wide range of characteristics, including external factors such as your age, race, gender, physical appearance and posture, and internal factors such as your accent, voice, language, culture and moral character. Ask a friend that you respect or a coach to critique you on your external factors. While you can't do much to change your age, race and gender you can do a lot to improve your grooming and posture. Practice authenticity in expressing your internal factors. While your external characteristics get you in the door, your internal characteristics give you the staying power to succeed.

Do the Work that Plays
to Your Strengths

Your Elemental traits are your innate talents and abilities that can be applied across any profession or industry, so no matter what job you currently have you can excel and succeed by playing to your strengths. Knowing your weaknesses is equally important as it can help you avoid being in situations that do not leverage your strong suit. For example, let's say that you are a Water person, currently in a management position. You may be doing fine or you may be floundering because you dislike holding people accountable and telling them when they fail to meet targeted goals. This is an opportunity for you to think about how you can best contribute to the calling while fulfilling your purpose. Ask yourself, "What are the activities that best express my gifts—my talents, skills, experiences and Elemental personality?" In the above situation, it may be that you enjoy strategic planning, consulting or executive coaching because it taps into your Water Element's natural contemplative, thoughtful and strategic proficiencies. Volunteer to facilitate the next strategic planning session for a department or the organization and see where it takes you!

Synergy Between Men
and Women in Business

Men and women are different in the way their brains work; men are often more linear in thinking and efficiency driven, while women are typically more holistic, empathetic and relationship-focused. In an era of incessant drive to increase productivity and efficiency, the competitive edge is evaporating as more companies become ever more similar in their processes. The unique differentiator for companies today is the relationship with their customers. Understanding, anticipating and conversing about customer's needs is paramount—all the qualities that are innate in the way women's brain operate. Men and women complement each other and when you bring synergy between the two you'll have both efficiency and empathy.

Love What You Do
Start Your Own Business

It may not be possible to find a job that fulfills your life purpose, makes use of your talents and is one that you are passionate about. Sometimes the best thing to do is to start your own business. Studies show that 61 percent of Americans want to be their own boss. The percentage is even higher among people in their twenties—a recent University of Phoenix survey found that 63 percent of twenty-somethings either owned their own businesses or wanted to someday. It's uplifting to see that the younger generation believes in doing work that is meaningful, has an impact beyond their own lives and makes them happy.

Here are the five fundamentals to increase the chance of success with your start-up:

1. Know
Your Gifts

Achieving success in any new endeavor requires dedicated commitment, discipline, hard work and single-minded focus while being open to change and opportunities. The first step is to know who you are (the gift), why you are here (to offer your giftedness) and how you want to actualize your potential (in delivering your gift to the word). Throughout this book you have learned about your Element personality, passion or life purpose and now it is time to put it all to good use. Ask and write down the answers to the following questions:

1) What is my Element/Personality Type?
2) What is my life purpose beyond myself?
3) If I didn't have to work to make a living, what would I be doing and how will those dreams help me fulfill my life purpose?
4) How can I use my abilities and talent to serve others and who will benefit from my dreams?
5) When I fast forward my dream to the end and look back, what do I wish to see?

(For sample answers to these questions please see the Appendix)

2. Make a
Road Map

When embarking on a journey you must map it out
and prepare a plan in advance. Starting a business is
no different. A business plan allows you to prepare for
and anticipate the various opportunities, challenges,
ups and downs. It also helps you assess your business's
strengths, or competitive advantage, and weaknesses
where you may need to ask for help and expertise
from others. Finally, a business plan reflects your value
system, passion and dreams that have been translated
into realistic, concrete and attainable steps. An ideal
business plan should include the following components:
Business concept, revenue model, strategy and plan for
carrying it out, your offering and competitive advantage,
your customers and competition, key players, financing
needs and finally an executive summary. There are free
business plan templates available on the Internet, but
you may want to hire a business coach or advisor to
help you if you are new to the process.

3. Roll Out
and Shout Out

Once you have completed your business plan and all
related components, you are ready to roll out. If you
are the Wood personality you may have been impatient
and wanting to start yesterday. If you are the Fire person
you have been filled with excitement from day one. If
you are the Earth type you may have spent a lot of time
worrying about your impending start up. If you are the
Metal type you may have wanted more time to perfect
your business plan and to wait until you felt perfectly
comfortable and ready. If you are the Water type you
may be dragging your feet or going by intuition rather
than a sophisticated business plan. The important
next step is: just do it! And do it with gusto by telling
everyone what you are doing, including your family,
friends, neighbors, co-workers, social networks, hair
stylist, online blogs, chat rooms and even strangers that
you meet. Your energy is infectious so give a shout out!

4. Adjust
and Refuel

Once you are over the initial startup phase and are more comfortable and settled in your daily work, the task is to continually improve, refine and elevate your skills. Be sure to closely track the market conditions and customer feedback and adjust your products, services and business processes accordingly. This activity should be ongoing so that you constantly stay relevant and meet the needs of your target market. Since you spend the bulk of your waking hours working, make sure that it continues to be enjoyable and meaningful to you. Moreover, prevent burnout and schedule regular periods for contemplation and retreat. As in a car race, you need to pull into the pit stop regularly to change the tires, replace damaged parts, make mechanical adjustments and refuel—so that you can get back out on the tracks as quickly and effectively as possible.

5. Exit or Keep
On Going

Like the seasons, every business has its cycles. Every
company in the world has gone through good and bad
times, up and down cycles, and profit and loss. Some
businesses are passed down from one generation to
the next, sometimes for several decades. You might find
yourself in a family business or know someone who
is. Chances are, you are experiencing mixed feelings if
you do not share your ancestor's founding vision. Why?
Because, simply put, you are not the same person as
the original founder of the business. This is probably
the reason why American businesses rarely pass down
beyond three successive generations. Having said that,
you may identify strongly with the original founding
mission of your ancestors and wish to continue their
legacy with passion and commitment. I am lucky that I
did.

Begin With
the End in Mind

There is nothing wrong with being true to your own life's purpose. In fact it is imperative that if you want health and happiness you need to align your life to your purpose. That also means if you start a business you need to have the end in mind right at the beginning. Ask yourself, "At what point do you want to exit the business by selling, take it public, merging or closing?" It may be that you would like to retire by a certain age, try your hand at a new endeavor, or you may have other personal goals. There is no right or wrong answer, just a sense of how long you would like to keep doing what you are doing. You may be surprised to find that you are enjoying what you are already doing, it is meaningful and congruent with your purpose, and that you are living your dream life—in which case, keep going!

In the following pages you will explore the range of work and careers that are compatible with your Element.

Wood Element
Career Possibilities

As a Wood Elemental person, your natural affinity for leadership makes you particularly suited for management and administration, teaching, or coaching. Politics, law enforcement and military service are also careers that could appeal to you. In general, Wood people excel in the natural sciences such as biology, botany, and environmental science. Careers that are aligned with tree products, such as lumber and paper mills, furniture design and manufacturing, house building, and paper products would also appeal to your natural Elemental inclinations.

Farming, food production and gardening are all near your soul, and so are landscape and environmental design. Your budding creativity is well suited to creative writing, interior design, photography and illustration. Because of your sense of justice and spiritual sensitivity, you are also suited to religious or charitable works. With your drive to push projects through to completion, you might also consider project management, publishing, software design or research and development. In the athletic arena, teaching or participating in sports, yoga, martial arts and dance are naturals for your Wood energy.

Fire Element
Career Possibilities

Your exuberance and love of attention makes you a natural for the performing arts, including film, theater, opera and comedy. You are charismatic and a natural born speaker so you might enjoy professional speaking, motivational coaching, sales, marketing, politics, public relations, advertising, diplomacy or managing others, while your creativity is a good match for visual, tactile and musical arts. You naturally spark in retail design, fashion, graphic design, commerce and tourism. Brokering, whether in art, stocks or real estate comes naturally to you, as does client representation in entertainment, sports or the arts.

As a Fire person, your heart and spirit are closely intertwined, so you could also find happiness in a religious, spiritual or teaching career. Medicine and healthcare would allow you an outlet for your compassion and wisdom. Your energy is robust, so the fitness and personal training industry would be an appropriate avenue for you. You might also want to consider psychology, social work and counseling; all tapping into your compassionate and empathetic heart.

Earth Element
Career Possibilities

Earth is grounded, nurturing and community oriented, which makes you a natural for customer service, teaching and service groups, or healing professions such as a physician, nurse, physical therapist, holistic practitioner, nutritionist, veterinarian or missionary. Construction and mining industries, civil engineering, infrastructure building, road building and earth-moving industries are natural outlets for your elemental energy, as are hobbies like pottery, ceramics, rock collecting, gemstones, and gardening.

As a nurturer, you are well suited for the hospitality industry, including restaurateur, hotelier and catering. Your love of food may help translate into careers as vintner, brewer, chef, gourmet products supplier and importer, snack producer, beverage maker, food and wine critic or agro-tourism guide. Real estate development and management and environmental and recycling services are also all potentially good fits for your energy. Industries that encourage participation in outdoor activities such as hiking, wilderness trekking, rock climbing and cycling are deeply instinctive for you.

Metal Element
Career Possibilities

Your meticulous and methodical nature makes you suited for careers in finance, accounting and technology. Numbers and data come naturally to your perfectionist instincts, and your strong logic and analytical knack means you will do well in data analysis and research. Technology, including hardware and software development, engineering and programming shall serve you well. All types of engineering match your Metal Element energy, including mechanical, electrical, chemical, systems and computer engineering.

Because you are interested and talented in trends, style and aesthetics, you might enjoy working in design, whether it's fashion, automotive, interior, watchmaking or architectural. Your love of scent and beauty could push you toward a career in cosmetics, consumer products, floral design or art dealing and curating. Your love of precious metals makes gemology and jewelry design of particular interest, and you could also find satisfaction in process-oriented work including robotics, regulatory agencies, compliance, appraising and software testing.

Water Element
Career Possibilities

Your power as a Water Element person comes from your vision and ability to create or conceive, so it would be wise to look for a career that takes advantage of your natural contemplative and self-sufficient temperament. As a Water Element person, you might enjoy work that is associated with movement of people or goods that come and go. In the Five Element paradigm, your Element excels at work that is involved with commercial trading and monetary exchanges, banking, investments, retail and international business. Transportation is energetically appropriate for you, such as airlines, sea and land transportation, shipping, delivery and import/export. Travel and tourism also appear in this same category of movement and mobility.

Your Water energy will also find satisfying expression in a wide variety of water industries, professions and functions including hydrology, water conservation, flood control, dam operation, usage management and treatment, and irrigation. Beverages are a big area for your exploration as is the distribution of solar panels, glass or crystal. As a keeper of timeless wisdom you are probably interested in culture and heritage, so you are well suited for a career in anthropology, art and museum curating and collecting or genealogy. Water persons are active and forward moving so you might consider a career in sports or coaching; in the realm of service, you could consider the legal field, consulting, human resources, medicine, media, education, healing and health care. Your artistic energy is a natural for drawing, painting, sculpture, film and photography. Contemplation also comes naturally to you so the study of philosophy shall bring fulfillment.

Part Three

Your Dreams and Wishes

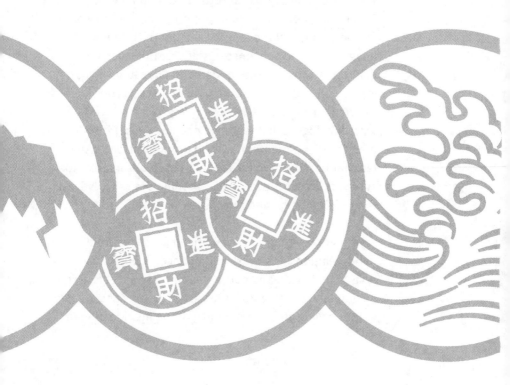

Once your core Element is revealed, and you learn about its profound impact on all aspects of your life, then you are ready to discover or re-affirm your life's purpose. You are ready to align with your passion, and embark on a journey to manifest your dreams. The refrain I often hear is, "I will be happy when my dreams come true!" Every person has dreams for his or her life, because they fulfill the fundamental human desire to be important, to make an impact, to feel valued, and to leave a legacy.

There is absolutely no value judgment about dreams. Dreams are personal, and therefore, you have complete freedom to travel the lengths and depths that your imagination and subconscious desire. However, you might first consider the fundamental question—what is your life purpose? In other words, what is your raison d'être—your reason for being here? I work with oncologists in integrative oncology and with many cancer patients. The most wonderful, and truly fascinating, common thread that I have observed among survivors is that they all had a burning desire to live out their life's mission and purpose.

Your vision for your life must encompass your body, mind, relationships, work and finances. Unless it is holistic, balanced and addresses all these aspects, it is incomplete. Coming up with a list of dreams and wishes before having an understanding of the mission of your life is akin to setting sail without a compass—you might have to backtrack, get lost, or worse, end up where you do not want to be. Discovering clarity of purpose helps you connect your goals and dreams with why they matter to you. Once you have your list, then it's about manifesting your life from vision to reality.

Benjamin Franklin once said, "If you fail to plan, you plan to fail." Your planning process may benefit immensely from using a time-tested, coaching system based on the wisdom of the I-Ching and the Five Elements. In an effort to help elucidate and guide you, we have created "Infinichi Coaching." Infinichi can greatly assist and facilitate the successful expression of your plans.

In the following chapters you will be guided through the Infinichi Coaching system, mapping out your destination though your life's purpose, passions and goals. You will learn to inventory the resources that you need, both material and human, in order to launch your journey. Once you begin on this path, you will leverage your Elemental strengths and work on improving your weaknesses. You will identify and remove blockages. Flow will occur, at times seemingly magically.

Along the way you will learn to stay on your path, and hold yourself accountable for your actions, progress and changes. You will be asked periodically to reassess and recommit to your purpose and mission—to renew and revitalize yourself—and then share the wisdom and experiences you've gained with others. One satisfying definition of success that we've all heard, but sometimes don't practice is helping others to achieve their goals and dreams. When we assist others in living healthy, happy and meaningful lives by sharing, mentoring and coaching, it fulfills the human need to have an impact.

As you journey through your life, Infinichi Coaching can help facilitate the fulfillment of your dreams, which may include evolving spiritually, improving your health, experiencing profound joy, finding meaning in your work, healing your relationships, taking care of our planet for future generations, becoming financially independent, and, ultimately, leaving a positive legacy that will live on.

Martin Luther King's momentous speech began with, "I have a dream..." and his actions changed the course of history in America and around the world. He left his indelible legacy.

Ready to get started with your dreams?

Chapter 11
Map Out Your Destination

All you need is the plan, the road map, and the courage to press on to your destination.

Earl Nightingale

Two Parts
to Your Life Purpose

There are two parts to your life purpose. Part one: - You have brought a gift to the world, and that gift is YOU, with all your unique potential, just as you are. Perfectly imperfect, and a work in progress. Your life purpose, should you choose to accept it, is to actualize your full potential.

The second part of your life purpose is beyond yourself. Look inwards and ask, "Why am I here, at this time, in this place, with this family, among this network of people, witness this suffering and pain, experiencing this good fortune?" Possibly the most important question you should ask, as taught by sages throughout time, is, "How do I plan to serve?" That is the purpose of your life. Think about it. Take some time, and write down your answers, now.

Passion Emanates
From the Heart

Oftentimes it is hard to come up with the purpose of your life just like that. Don't worry if you can't do it just yet. Relax, sit back and let your mind stop. Your mind is like a monkey that likes to jump from branch to branch and tree to tree, never stopping long enough for you to grasp it with clarity and certainty. Instead, tap into your heart and allow the passion to flow. Remember the moments when you fell deeply in love, your passion was unstoppable, and nothing could have stood in the way of you expressing your profound love. What would happen if you applied that same passion to the work that you are already doing? What would happen to your relationships if you rekindled the fire with your loved ones? What if you opened your heart and started experiencing compassion, deeper meaning, and connection? Ask yourself, "If I don't have to work to make a living today what would I be passionately doing?" Write down your answers now.

What Do You See When You
Fast Forward Your Life to the End

Life is short and fleeting. You've heard the crotchety gripe, "Yesterday I was a young man full of ideals, and now I am old and cynical. Where did my life go?" Don't let this be you. No matter your age, it's never too late to discover your passion and life purpose, and manifest your dreams. The shame would be to never know and experience a life that is meaningful and fulfilling for you. Why is it that "no one on their death-bed wished they had spent another day at the office?" Ask yourself, "When I fast forward my life to the end and reflect back on my entire life, what do I wish to see?" Write down your answers now.

(For sample answers to these questions please see the Appendix)

Decision-Making
Made Easy

Once you have a clarity of purpose for your life, it makes decision-making that much easier. It will be the True North for your journey. It will help you evaluate whether something that comes along positively facilitates, potentially detracts, or may cause you to detour away from your destination. Whenever you are confronted with the need to choose your involvement in something, ask yourself, "Does this decision positively facilitate my life purpose?" If the answer is yes, then if you have the time and energy, you should get involved. If the answer is no, move on.

Dreams are Powerful Because
They Can Change the World

Gandhi's dream of independence for his people peacefully liberated India from Britain. Likewise, Mandela held steadfast to his dreams despite being incarcerated for many years, finally bringing down apartheid in South Africa. Major milestones, innovations and revolutions in human history all began with one person's dream. Dreams are powerful because they can potentially change the world. So, to borrow from one of the finest speeches in history...you have a dream...

Tales of
Two Dreams

There are two types of dreams—fleeting and enduring. Fleeting dreams are more like desires. They arise from emotional or physical needs and cravings. Enduring dreams, on the other hand, tend to be meaningful to you and are often related to your life purpose or about building and leaving a legacy. For instance, if you want to lose 10 pounds so that you can fit into that bikini in time for summer, you may diet like crazy and succeed at losing the weight. Eventually though, you regain all the weight you lost, perhaps even before the summer is over. This would be a fleeting dream. In contrast, you may have dreams to achieve good health, stay physically active and make consistent, positive changes to your diet, exercise and lifestyle, because part of your life purpose is to stay fit and active. This, in a simplistic illustration, would be an enduring dream.

Dreams Are Personal
Because They Are Your Own

Dreams are personal and therefore you have the complete freedom to choose what they may be. You shouldn't feel compelled to have dreams of saving the world or something else equally grand, or else your dream is not worthwhile. Ideally your dreams should be in alignment with your passion and life purpose, because dreams are the vehicle through which you realize and actualize this purpose.

Answer the following questions: 1) How can I use my abilities and talents to serve? 2) Who will benefit from my dreams? 3) Will my dreams help me fulfill my life purpose? You do not need to rush. Take some time to write down your answers.

Some Dreams
Are Universal

John Lennon once wrote, "Imagine there's no countries, it isn't hard to do, nothing to kill or die for, and no religion too, imagine all the people living life in peace..." He was a brilliant songwriter and musician who actualized his unique potential by sharing his messages with the world through his timeless music. His life was cut short, but his legacy became enormous, influencing an entire generation around the world. John wanted to promote love, peace and harmony everywhere he went. That was his purpose. The music was his passion and vehicle to do so. He went on in the song, "You may say I'm a dreamer but I'm not the only one, I hope someday you'll join us and the world will be as one." Some dreams are universal.

Goals are the Stepping Stones
to Your Dreams

If your purpose is to shelter and protect your loved ones, and you are passionate and talented in carpentry, you may dream of building a house. To manifest this dream, you must set goals, an architectural blueprint, that shows all the steps necessary to building it. Goals are the stepping stones toward your dreams. Many people are used to setting goals or resolutions. However, how often have you heard something like, "I never keep my resolutions past January." Most people quickly throw in the towel. To increase the probability of success, goals should be based on a deeper purpose, or passionate vision. Goals must be realistic and bite-sized, so that they are achievable. Goals must be matched with adequate resources, whether it's people, money or circumstance, and they must also be measurable. Finally, we need to be held accountable for meeting our goals. Goals are the building blocks of your dreams.

The Importance of Defining
the "Why" of Your Goals

One of the hardest goals for most people to achieve
is losing a desirable amount of weight within a certain
timeframe. Weight loss may be the goal, but where
people fail is defining the purpose of "why" they
want to lose weight. If your life purpose is to actualize
your full potential, and your goal is to stay around
and be healthy for your children and grandchildren,
then getting heart disease would cut short your life's
potential. Therefore, a goal of achieving better physical
health and reducing heart disease risk would be strongly
supported. In fact, if your focus is on becoming fitter
and stronger, the goal may naturally change to more
regular exercise and healthier eating. The weight
loss goal turns out to be secondary while increasing
muscle, decreasing fat and cholesterol, and boosting
cardiovascular capacity becomes the primary objective.
My good friend Ramona Capello's father died of heart
disease. For her it became a personal mission to prevent
it and to help others achieve the same goal. To that end,
besides changing her own diet and lifestyle, she started
Corazona Foods (Corazona means "heart" in Italian),
offering oatmeal bars containing cholesterol-lowering
plant sterols. It became wildly successful. You will be
more successful when you connect your goals to your
purpose.

Connect Your Goals
to a Personal Mission

If in fact, achieving weight wellness is your primary goal, you'll have more success in accomplishing it by connecting it to a passion. For example, let's say you have a passion for cooking. Challenge yourself to be innovative and go beyond the usual high calorie comfort food that you are used to preparing daily. Transition to new, low calorie, nutritious and tasty recipes. Research and compile new recipes. Ask friends or co-workers to share the recipes that work for them. Try cooking without certain ingredients like dairy, sugar, and gluten. Find healthy, lower calorie substitutes and be creative with your cooking. Another good friend, Lizanne Falsetto, founded the highly successful company behind ThinkThin Bars by combining her love of cooking with a desire to stay healthy on the road as a busy fashion model. Today she is gorgeous, fit and successful as she passionately helps millions of people achieve wellness.

Make Your Goals
Bite-Sized

To make your goals realistic, start with small changes. Instead of drastic changes that are usually unsustainable, choose to cut out only one ingredient that you normally use in your food preparation two days a week. For example, during week one, substitute olive oil or grapeseed oil for the usual butter on Mondays and Wednesdays. Then on week two, expand that to Monday through Thursday. And finally on week three, completely eliminate butter and try incorporating new oils like avocado oil and sesame oil. If you do things gradually, you don't feel "deprived", or "punished" by your new, healthier diet. After succeeding in eliminating butter from your diet you might want to choose sugar as the next item to eliminate, finding healthy substitutes like Stevia, a natural calorie-free plant sweetener or luo han guo, a fruit sweetener used in China that's 200 times sweeter than sugar without much calories—yeah, you heard it right! 200 times sweeter AND less calories! Both are completely safe, unlike artificial sweeteners. This is great news for those with a sweet tooth. So, moral of the story? Make your goals bite-sized, and therefore doable and sustainable.

Assess Your Needs
Before You Go

Understanding your Element type helps you assess your strengths and weaknesses and the potential blocks along your path to reaching your destination. Before undertaking any journey, for example, a climbing expedition, it's important to be well prepared with a good map and adequate resources and supplies. Apply this simple, common-sense approach to your own life challenges and journeys. Make a checklist of what you need, both materially and otherwise in order to maximize success. The checklist should include the following: 1) your strengths that will help you, 2) your weaknesses and blind spots that may potentially hinder you, 3) the resources and support that you need, 4) the time and energy that you have to devote to it, and finally 5) the risks and rewards. Write these down and carefully deliberate them. Make sure it is a goal that you truly want to achieve.

Unleash Your
Inner Surfer

Leveraging your strengths in life is like surfing. With a quick paddle to catch the wave, the swell will naturally carry you and your board some distance. Any surfer will tell you the feeling of riding a wave is highly exhilarating, and for some people, it is almost like a religious experience. Your Elemental strengths consist of traits that you were either born with or have cultivated through practice. These traits are like the swells in the ocean that push your board along, giving you a natural boost. For example the Metal Element/Methodical Type is naturally organized and meticulous. If your pursuit is to become a good bookkeeper, you merely have to let your natural gifts and strengths shine. Coupled with professional accounting and bookkeeping skills, you will succeed much more easily due to your Elemental traits. Write down your strengths and what you learned about your Element from Part One of this book and unleash the inner surfer in you.

A Good Coach
Is an Invaluable Resource

A critical aspect of goal setting is to evaluate the resources and support that are available to you. These resources include people who've been on the same path before—they know which pitfalls and hidden dangers to avoid. Seek out the experts, and ask for their advice. Sound advice may save you time, energy and money and possibly even your life. Similarly a good life coach, such as an Infinichi Coach, can help you identify the uneven terrain on your journey, and help you to navigate around obstacles and reach your destination.

Use Your Time
Wisely

The two things most people take for granted are time and energy. The old saying "youth is wasted on the young" testifies to the regrets about wasted time from those in midlife and beyond. Media companies constantly seduce you to fork over your precious time to consume their programming, and on average Americans watch five hours of TV per day, according to Nielsen Reports. Unfortunately, time is a diminishing asset that starts counting down as soon as you are born. On the positive side, the beauty is that you can absolutely choose how you spend your time or make time for what matters to you—whether it's to engage in work that is in alignment with your life purpose, enjoy a leisure activity, or spend it with your friends and loved ones. No matter how old you are, it's never too late—use your time wisely.

Breath, Flow and Roll
with the Punches

Don't get frustrated when things don't pan out according to your plans. It happens. As long as you know your destination, there are multiple ways of getting to it. Plans are guidelines and not set in stone, so if they don't fit the circumstances, change them. Cultivate the ability to adapt to life's unexpected hurdles. Wood and Metal Element people in particular may react negatively to unforeseen obstacles. Breathe, flow and roll with the punches, but don't lose sight of where you are going. The reason many species on our planet have died out is that they failed to adapt to the changing environment. Humans thrived because of the instinctive ability to adapt. Enjoy your journey and change your plans if you need to. As John Lennon said, "Life is what happens while you're busy making other plans."

Gather
Your Life Force Energy

As a clinician, I regularly see patients who complain of tiredness and not having enough energy to do what they want to do. It's a challenge to achieve your dreams with a lack of energy or life force. Some patients have conditions that rob them of energy such as chronic fatigue syndrome, autoimmune disease and anemia. Others have depression, anxiety and apathy that also affect one's energy. Work with your mind-body healthcare practitioners and discover the reason for your low vitality and work on restoring it for the sake of achieving your potential.

Imbalance Within Your Five
Elements Can Affect Your Energy

In Chinese medicine, energy or chi (qi) is also called life force. Any imbalances within your Five Elements organ network can upset your energy. Each Element is represented by an organ system. If your Wood Element/ liver network is off balance, then your ability to detoxify is impaired, leading to toxic overload and fatigue. If your Fire Element/heart network is under stress, then your cardiovascular circulation becomes inadequate, depriving your cells of blood flow. If your Earth Element/ spleen-stomach network is weakened, your ability to digest and absorb nutrients is compromised, and therefore, your energy will be sluggish. If your Metal Element/lung network is insufficient, then your body will be deficient in oxygen. Finally, if your Water Element/kidney-adrenal network is exhausted, then your hormonal functions will be lacking, resulting in low energy. Enhance your energy with the special herbal supplements of Five Elements plus the individual Elements. When necessary, seek help from a doctor of acupuncture. In my many years of personal and generational experience, Chinese medicine helps restore and gather up your chi.

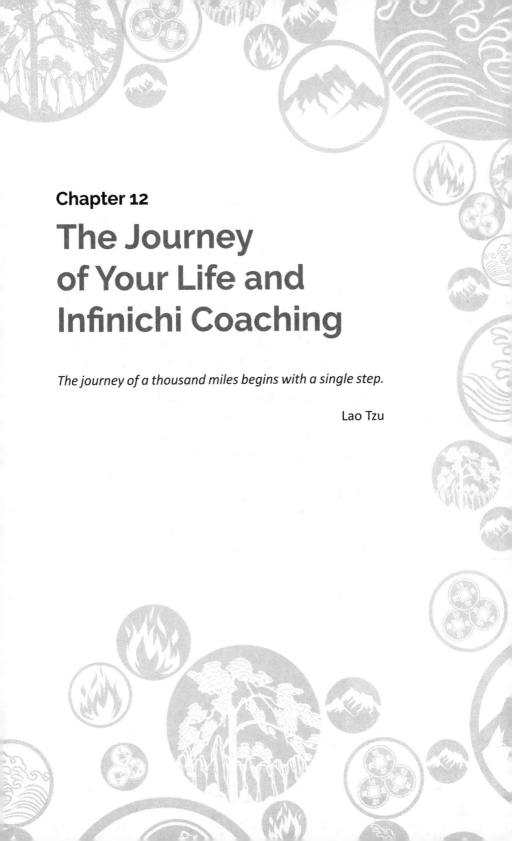

Chapter 12

The Journey of Your Life and Infinichi Coaching

The journey of a thousand miles begins with a single step.

Lao Tzu

Inertia Is the Enemy
of an Actualized Life

Advancements in human civilization have been due in large part to migration and the resulting exchange of knowledge, goods and information across the globe. Since early human history, migration was necessary for survival. A journey was an unpredictable adventure that was at once perilous and lucrative. Besides material gains, specialized knowledge was highly sought after and invaluable to those who possessed it.

Your entire life can be likened to a long, continuous journey from beginning to end. Once you've decided on your destination, planned and prepared for your trip, it's time to launch your expedition. Inertia is the enemy of an actualized life. Many people only dream of a life that's different than the one they inhabit and are too paralyzed by fear and inertia to do anything about it.

Break Through Fear and Inertia
with Your Elemental Strengths

What is stopping you from taking your first step towards realizing your dreams? For most people it is the fear of change, which is understandable. It is rooted in the primal desire for stability, predictability and permanence that arose from the hunter-gatherer, nomadic experiences of the human past. However, if you find yourself unhappy, unfulfilled and unhealthy in your current situation and yet do not have the courage to change, ask yourself, "What is the cost of remaining in the status quo?" Will you have any regrets at the end of your life? It does consume more fuel for a car, boat or airplane to go from standing still to moving but it takes a lot less fuel to maintain motion. Similarly, it requires more energy to take that first step in your journey but once you do, staying on the path requires less energy to sustain.

Use your Elemental traits to help you break through inertia. For example if you are Wood Element, use your strong drive, if you are Fire, stoke your passion, if you are Earth focus on the rewards, if you are Metal, appeal to your logic, and finally if you are Water, tap your intuition.

Creating Value
in Helping Another Person

As you have discovered and learned about your core
Element, I hope that you have come to appreciate
the strengths and gifts you possess that create value
for another person. For example if you are a Wood/
Authoritative personality, your inborn leadership
emboldens you to right wrongs, break down barriers to
equality, and do whatever it takes to make meaningful
things happen for others. Fire/Passionate personalities
inspire others with their principles and beliefs, helping
them to make better choices and to feel special,
loved, and connected. Earth/Caring individuals bestow
compassion, service and loving care, which extend
into building supportive teams and systems. Metal/
Methodical personalities excel at developing rules,
structures and processes that facilitate achievement and
success. A Water/Wise person is someone who helps
create clarity, advance innovations and turn crisis into
opportunities that improve lives for others.

Tips for
Wood Element Type

Because you are naturally endowed with a strong drive, once you are clear in your mind about your destination or goals you have less of an issue initiating your journey. Not only are you goal-driven, you also have the ability to marshal the resources and people necessary to meet your goal. You are prone, however, to being flummoxed when situations go awry or when people fail to perform to your expectations. The frustration can turn into an aggressive forcefulness that can potentially destroy the goodwill and morale of your team. Cultivate the adaptable, go-with-the-flow qualities of the Water Element. Prepare for and be open to taking detours instead of the tendency to demolish what gets in your way.

Tips for
Fire Element Type

Your natural ability to inspire others with your vision and passion helps you with any new initiative. Connecting with people comes easy to you, as is motivating them to join your cause. What you may want to lookout for is the risk of flaming out before the task is complete, as you are often full of passion at the beginning of an endeavor but see it wane or move on to the next cause. Therefore your challenge is to stay the course and persevere through any difficulties. Cultivate the Wood Personality trait of determination and persistence, and when you start to feel the edges burning out, re-energize yourself with the original purpose and intent of the quest.

Tips for
Earth Element Type

Faithful, steady and continual progress is the trademark of the Earth Element. You are the person that everyone can count on because of your caring, nurturing and selfless nature. The challenge you may face is getting started. Your penchant is to tend to other people's needs before your own, so working on your own needs, path or project is slow going at best. You would be best to develop the passion of the Fire Element and the urgency of the Wood Personality so that you can commence on your own journey. Once you are progressing down your path, you can tap into your trusting and constant nature to keep you on track.

Tips for
Metal Element Type

Your tendency to be careful, meticulous and comprehensive increases your likelihood to succeed. On the flip side, you may be prone to over planning, to the point where you become bogged down by too much data and information. Let go of the need to control the outcome and instead cultivate the trusting nature of the Earth Element—have faith that with clarity of purpose and a plan that's good enough in hand, you will eventually get to where you want to go. Make room in your plan for spontaneity and adaptability, as sometimes the best experiences in life come from the unexpected.

Tips for
Water Element Type

Being intuitive, contemplative and low key come naturally to you, the Water Element/Wise person. Your conservative and discrete predisposition keeps your goals, agenda and plans hidden from others, so it may be more challenging to enlist help to pilot your ship as you set sail for your destination. You may also fear the unknown, and if you allow this trepidation to settle in you might find yourself paralyzed and unable to take action. Likewise, your tendency to go with the flow may allow the currents to take you too far off course and end up in a different place than you originally intended. Worry not, as the Water Personality is adaptable and agile in reformulating alternate ways. Eventually you will reach your destination. You may benefit, however, from borrowing from the Metal Element's methodical planning in order to avoid frustration and floundering.

Let the Journey
Begin

Your life is a journey so let it begin. We take traveling for granted today in an age when one can circle the globe in 48 hours. Unlike our ancestors who traveled from one continent to another on years-long caravan trips filled with challenges, today I can have breakfast in Buenos Aires and dinner with my family in Los Angeles, all without much of a thought. The pace of life and the flow of information have also sped up, leaving us breathless, overloaded and longing for a simpler, slower time. Decide the pace of your journey and build in time to stop, reflect and recharge as you progress toward your next destination.

People Work at Dying,
They Don't Work at Living

The last time I saw Jack Lalanne he was in his early 90s, still fit and working out two hours a day. He joked that he hated dying because it would ruin his image. Jack was very clear about his life's purpose early on, which was to help people through prevention. At age 21, he opened the nation's first health and fitness club in Oakland, California, where he offered supervised weight and exercise training and nutrition advice. Jack decided that the best way for him to succeed in realizing his mission was to passionately embody it in his own life. He maintained a healthy lifestyle, often training for feats and stunts that demonstrated his incredible vitality. Even in his 60s, he swam the entire length of the Golden Gate Bridge underwater and handcuffed. Jack was happily married for over 50 years. He impacted many people's lives through his TV shows. "People work at dying," he said, "they don't work at living. My workout is my obligation to life." Jack died at age 96 and lived a fully actualized life.

Are You Packed
for Your Journey?

People are often unprepared for the journey they are undertaking. Some people bring what they don't need and leave what they need behind. Fortunately you may be one of those people that start with a checklist. That's good. Take an inventory of what you need and then decide if you already possess the items or will have to obtain them. Write down the answers to the following questions: What are the essential ingredients I need, both within and without to achieve my goals? Whose expertise, skills and advice do I need to get me there? What may stand in the way of me reaching my destination? Record the answers to these questions in your journal now.

Commitment
One Day At a Time

Perceive your life purpose as a gift you give to the world each day. You have special talents and gifts that when expressed through your core Elemental personality allows you to live purposefully each and everyday. To live a purposeful life requires commitment. It's certainly easier to just forget about it all and go back to your old pattern of work, TV watching, Internet surfing, fitful sleep, weekend debauchery and then repeat. If you want a meaningful life, how do you find the strength and endurance for a life-long commitment? It seems overwhelming, doesn't it? The secret lies in affirmation and dedication one day at a time. You see, most people can handle devotion for a day but not many can promise devotion for a lifetime. At the start of your day, use this following invocation to strengthen your resolve to an authentic life:

Dear Divine Universe,
Creator of my being and giver of this life,

I am thankful for the opportunity to be here.
Today please give me strength
So that I may be authentic and live a purposeful life
By offering my gift to the world and being of service to another person.
I am forever grateful.
Thank you

Restore and Rejuvenate
at the Root

It's normal to get tired on your journey called life. It's also entirely too tempting to reach for stimulants to keep you going, such as pills to help you stay up all night studying or driving. These stimulants, while temporarily useful, actually harm you over time with many potential side effects, not to mention addiction. Multibillion-dollar businesses have been built on pumping people up so they can keep pushing their tired bodies and minds past healthy limits. The side effects of common stimulants like caffeine includes high blood pressure, sleep disorders, palpitations, anxiety, panic attacks, elevated blood sugar, dehydration, diarrhea, frequent urination, withdrawal headaches, acid reflux, fibrocystic diseases of the breasts and uterus, and the list goes on and on.

Besides adequate rest and relaxation, along with good nutrition and a supportive cadre of family, friends and community, wise Chinese sages long ago devised natural botanical formulations of potent life force-boosting herbs to help support healthy functions and vigorous energy. It's important to restore and rejuvenate at the root, and not just address the symptoms of the energy depletion.

Kids Have
Missions Too

A friend's nine-year-old boy, Devon, loved dogs and
when he saw on TV that police dogs were being
shot, injured and killed while on duty he decided to
do something about it. He talked to the head of the
local police K-9 unit, veterinarians, the head of the
school he was attending and his parents and decided
that acquiring bulletproof vests specially designed for
police dogs offered the best protection against gunshot
deaths. The vests were expensive, however, and the
department simply did not have the budget for them.
Undeterred, Devon hatched a plan and enlisted all the
people that could help him to raise enough money to
buy the vests for the local police department's dogs.
Despite the long odds, he not only succeeded but also
brought awareness to the problem, since his story was
covered by the media and spread to other parts of the
country. Devon took inventory of what he needed, made
a plan, took action and enlisted help to achieve his goal.
Most importantly, his goals were measureable as the
death rate for police dogs wearing protective vests while
on duty plummeted dramatically after the vest program
started.

The Antidote to Procrastination
is Accountability

I get asked all the time, "Dr. Mao, how do you manage to do so much—a full time practice, a school of Chinese medicine, the dozens of books you've written, the international speaking tours, the TV appearances, and so on? What is your secret?" My answer is simple: Accountability. I am embarrassed to admit that I am a big procrastinator. It's true. But since I know my weakness I've actively tried to overcome it. I hold myself accountable to my patients by showing up to take care of them. I am accountable to my students by showing up to teach. I am accountable to my readers and publishers by writing my books (instead of watching TV).

You Show Up To Meet Someone
Else's Expectations Until You can
Do It for You

We've all been conditioned from early on to be
accountable to our teachers to complete our homework
assignments, accountable to our bosses to complete
the work we were hired to do, and accountable to
our life coaches to put effort into changes that we
agreed to. The list goes on and on. The important point
is to leverage the universal human desire to please
someone to help you get started. Ultimately the cure for
procrastination lies within you—being accountable to
your own conscience.

Performance
Scoreboard

If you are an athlete training for a marathon, you will want to monitor your pace with the objective of running faster in shorter periods of time. If you are an avid golfer you are constantly keeping score on your game, attempting to lower your handicap. Likewise, on your life path you need to monitor and keep score on how well you are performing relative to the goals you've set. A scoreboard can be a spreadsheet, a journal or a smartphone application with the sole purpose of keeping you on track. Whether it's about physical health, a financial goal, relationship healing or career advancement, keeping a written scoreboard can help you measure your progress impartially.

You Cannot Change
What You Cannot Measure

For instance, let's say one of your goals is to lower your blood sugar to reverse your type 2 diabetes. You start monitoring your fasting blood glucose each morning upon rising before you've eaten anything. As you implement your exercise, eating and stress reduction program you continue to monitor your sugar levels. Overtime you discover that you've lost weight, gotten in better physical shape and have become more serene; and correspondingly, you observed the drop in your fasting glucose to the point that you were able to work with your doctor on reducing or getting off of your medication entirely. Having had measurable glucose numbers helped you stay focused on your efforts, increasing your chance of success.

Earth Element's
Balanced Caring

One of my patients, Maria, is a two-time breast cancer
survivor. Part of her life's mission is to prevent the
return of cancer and to make a difference in the lives
of others diagnosed with breast cancer. She took
the Five Element Quiz and discovered that she's an
Earth Element with a Caring Personality. Naturally,
due to her Elemental strengths of consideration and
support she volunteered to accompany and transport
patients to their chemo and radiation treatments. As a
former chef, she also organized meal preparations and
home deliveries from the patients' friends as well as
other volunteers. She feels satisfied that she's able to
leverage her strengths to serve while at the same time
fulfilling her purpose. The flip side of her Earth Element
weakness is overextension and a tendency to over
commit, which has the potential to affect her health.
I advised that she delegate to more volunteers and
dedicate three half-days a week to the work instead of
the five to six half-days that she started out with. She is
now much happier and feels more balanced.

Take Small Steps
Instead of Big Leaps

As you travel on your journey, remember that it's a marathon and not a 100-yard dash. Try to conserve your energy and pace yourself, and most importantly take small, steady steps instead of big leaps. I remember my father telling me a story of his daily walks. He has walked at least one hour each day for most of his life. One day he was out walking and came to a ditch. Instead of taking a little more time out of the way to cross it at the narrow point he decided to leap across it. Unfortunately he landed on an uneven surface and sprained his ankle. It was badly injured and he had to be off of his feet for a good two weeks to nurse the healing before he was able to resume his walks. It was a humbling lesson for even a master.

Taking small steps means looking for small opportunities that offer a greater chance of success rather than big opportunities with a lower chance of success. Warren Buffet once said: "I don't look to jump over seven-foot bars; I look around for one foot bars that I can step over." With that guiding principle Buffet went on to become one of the richest people in the world.

Your Coach,
Your Personal Mentor

I've had the fortune of being coached by an incredibly accomplished master teacher, healer, author (of over 150 books) and mentor—Hua-Ching Ni or OmNi, who happened to be my father. Not only did he save my life when I was a child after I fell three stories and every specialist said I would be paralyzed for life and brain damaged, he has coached and guided me my entire life. My father has led an extraordinary life of learning, and as a result possessed keen insights and astonishing powers of intuition. He taught me the predictive arts and science of the I Ching and the Five Elements Personality that has helped me uncover my true nature and improve my deficiencies. It has also helped me overcome many obstacles in my life and to achieve health, joy, and abundance and fulfillment.

Infinichi
Coaching

I've been blessed to have a personal coach. It is precisely the reason why my brother and I, aside from our busy acupuncture and Chinese medicine practices, have also devoted our lives to Infinichi Coaching so that many more people may experience their own life transformations. There is no greater satisfaction than to see people go through their self-discovery, find their life purpose and begin on the path to living an authentic, joyful and purposeful life. I invite you to explore self-coaching with some of the techniques mentioned throughout this book and when you are ready for a personal mentor, like I have had, contact us at infinichi.com and start working with a certified Infinichi Coach today.

Conclusion

Share Your Successes, Leave Your Legacy

In a way, you achieve immortality through your legacy. Long after you are gone your offspring and the world shall remember you for your deeds. Your legacy shall inspire generations to wake up, to discover, to dream and to achieve the impossible.

May you live a long, healthy and happy life!

Dr. Mao Shing Ni

To have a healthy, happy and fulfilling life is a universal human desire. Such a life is defined by many attributes. By writing this book, I hope that I have helped you discover who you are through the ancient knowledge of the Five Elements. As you learned about yourself I hope that you also learned about how your Elemental Personality has created opportunities and challenges for you in different aspects of your life. As you find the purpose and mission for your life, and use the coaching tools to help you reach your goals and actualize your dreams, it is my hope that you will share your successes and legacy by helping others.

Now it is your turn to act, to fulfill your potential by applying the knowledge you have learned. In your quest to optimize who you are and find balance in your Five Elements, the holistic approach of this book can serve as your foundation. The most basic attribute for a fulfilling life is health. I highly suggest that you read my other books—Secrets of Longevity, Secrets of Self Healing and Second Spring. These books show you how to attain optimum health by decreasing disease risks through the combined wisdom of East and West. The time-tested traditions of the ancients coupled with scientific advancements of modern science are blended in this approach to health. Health and longevity are the base from which you can enjoy your life's true potential.

Be a Guide on the Road
Less Traveled

You've been down the road. You've seen the condition of the road, found the detours around the obstacles, and repaired and marked the road so that others can follow and benefit from your efforts and wisdom. You've taken the road less traveled and have glimpsed uncommon vistas. It's time to share with those who trail after by mentoring and coaching them.. By guiding others to discover their own gifts and helping them to manifest those unique talents, you are doing your part to uplift the world.

Service to Others
Opens Your Heart

There is no higher human endeavor than service to others in need. Studies show that those who regarded service as an important activity in their lives suffered less health problems and coped with stress more successfully than those who did not regard service as important. When you give of yourself you naturally increase the production of happy neurochemicals and literally open or dilate your blood vessels to your heart. Physiological benefits aside, in order for humanity to continue to evolve positively long after you are gone, you can to do your part today to lend a hand, uplift someone and bring joy to people's hearts and lives.

Make a Difference
Every Day

Twenty-something founder of NextDrop, Anu Sridharan from India, created a mobile app that provides real-time information on water availability in India via SMS (short message service). In addition to serving the needs of women in developing countries she has helped solve a problem of unreliable water delivery that affects 90 percent of Asia. Her endeavor is transforming the lives of countless families everyday. You don't have to wait to impact hundreds or thousands of people. When you wake up in the morning ask yourself, "What can I do to make a difference today in someone else's life?" And then go do it.

Give Health
by Building Stoves

In my travels throughout Latin America, I was fortunate to meet an extraordinary man, Stephen Miller, a former investment banker from Dallas, Texas. Miller started HELPS International in the mid-1980s in Guatemala to provide medical services to indigenous communities that lacked it. After repeatedly caring for lung diseases in many Guatemalan women, the main cause was discovered to be smoke inhalation from cooking indoors on open fires, which was common throughout the indigenous populations of Central America. With the help of designers and engineers, a simple but effective stove that properly vented the smoke through a chimney was created and provided by volunteers to many families. The consequence of this simple act was the gift of health to countless women and their families. I had the chance to participate in building stoves for families and was so deeply moved by the impact of such a simple act that afterwards I brought a group of my friends to volunteer in Guatemala. It felt good to give health by building stoves, besides delivering medical services.

Legacy Is a Consequence
of Beliefs and Actions

When I first sat down with Nancy Aossey, she had been asked to interview me for potential membership in a leadership organization. Instead, I interviewed her and was awed and fascinated by her vision, passion and action that empowered her to lead International Medical Corps for the last 30 years as its President and CEO. To date International Medical Corps has responded to every major disaster and delivered more than $2 billion in humanitarian relief and medical training in more than 70 countries, including the Ebola outbreak in West Africa. She didn't set out to create a legacy but through her beliefs and actions over a span of 30 years, she has in fact left an indelible impact on many lives.

The Golden
Thread

When asked how he managed to mediate between opposing beliefs systems and make people aware of their common humanity, Desmond Tutu, the Nobel Peace Prize Laureate and Archbishop Emeritus replied, "It doesn't matter where we worship or what we call God; there is only one, interdependent human family. We are born for goodness, to love—free of prejudice." He went on to say, "I don't believe in the notion of opposing belief systems. It would be more accurate to say that human beings have a long history of rationalizing acts of inhumanity on the basis of their own interpretations of the will of God." The golden thread that bridges the differences between religions is to treat others, as we would have them treat us. Or, conversely, not to treat anyone as we would ourselves not wish to be treated.

Become a Good Steward
of Our Planet

We only have one planet, so we have an obligation to take good care of it and leave it a better place than the way we found it. Akin to Noah's Ark, if the ship sinks we all go down together. You might be frustrated by the debates on climate change, and perhaps feel helpless and wonder what to do about it. Well here is a list of simple steps provided by Homer Robinson that you can act on today. 1. Switch from water cooler jugs to on-site water purifiers. 2. Ban plastic bottles; invest in stainless steel bottles branded for everyone. 3. Mandate double-sided printing. 4. Convert to LED lighting. 5. Install smart power strips. 6. Raise/lower your air conditioner/ heater thermostat setting by one or two degrees. 7. Install water aerators on taps to save water. 8. Put one or two liter, sealed water bottles in flush tanks of toilets to save water. 9. Create preferred parking spaces for encouraging carpooling. 10. Forego paper and plastic ware and install Energy Star dishwashers in offices so everyone is happy using the office flatware and dishes.

You Have the Power
to Be Happy

To take joy in everyday life is a blessing that is available
to all. It requires a strong desire and willingness to
change in order to create the joy you want. If you are
unhappy, choose to be otherwise. You have that power,
because no one can make you unhappy: only you
determine how you feel. Commit to infusing your life
and that of others with joy.

Love Is Fundamental
to All Life

To love and be loved is crucial, because love is fundamental to all life. It starts with the benevolent love from the universal divine or God. This love is expressed through maternal love toward children, and the goodness all human beings can feel toward one another as well as to all living and nonliving things. Love's alchemy brings about the attraction between two people that inspires them to come together and form a family—the building block of the eternal universe. It is also the feeling that causes people to grow and share in community, supporting one another in life.

True Freedom
Without Limits

Freedom is something taken for granted in the developed countries of the world. The basic freedoms to think, speak, and be are to be valued and preserved, as they allow us to develop as unique individuals, collectively making up the diverse world in which we live. Cultivate in your body freedom from illness, in your mind freedom from prejudice, and in your spirit freedom from the bondage of cults and fundamentalism—then you will taste true freedom without limit.

Goodwill Is Nutrition
for the Soul

Another basic attribute is prosperity, and this is meant in both the material and the nonmaterial sense. Material goods are necessary for a comfortable and secure life, and it is right to be motivated to work hard in exchange for a decent living. Being creative and productive benefits you and others. We also need intangible prosperity, or goodwill. Accumulating goodwill is part of human nature. Goodwill is like nutrition for the soul: the more you accrue, the more content you become.

Freedom to Choose
Your Life's Mission

Life without meaning is empty, but meaning is
something you must give your own life. It is not for
anyone else to tell you what your life is about. Take time
to explore and define your life's purpose. Is your life like
that of the ant scurrying about looking for food? Or of
a butterfly dancing amid blossoms without a care? Ants
and butterflies have their role to play in our planet's
ecology and in the universe. The difference between
humans and insects is the freedom to choose. What is
the role and purpose of your existence? When you find
that mission and commit your energy to it, your life will
be fulfilled.

Share Your
Wisdom

It has been said that everyone wants health and wisdom. Wisdom is not easily definable, yet everyone seeks it, regarding it as the highest human achievement. The funny thing is, wisdom usually does not appear until you are older, and yet no one wants to age. Wisdom is essential to achieving good health, and staying healthy in turn enables you to maximize your life span and acquire yet more wisdom. Through the continual lessons and practices of living a balanced and harmonious life, as well as cultivating your spirit, the wisdom in you grows with each passing day. And with it comes the obligation to share your wisdom in the form of service to others.

Clear the Blocks —
A Writer Gets Unstuck with Infinichi Coaching

Obstacles and blockages often show up uninvited. They can cause temporary holdup to your goals and dreams and sometimes leaving you feeling helplessly stuck. A blockage may be circumstantial, in which the external situation causes the distraction or interruption. Other times an obstacle is originated internally or self-created.

For instance, one of my patients dreamed of being a writer. He set a goal of finishing a novel in 12 months and prepared for the endeavor by committing to writing for an hour each day by going to the local Starbucks first thing in the morning and writing on his laptop. The first week he was able to go three days in a row, but then he had to travel for work the remainder of the week. The second week he was only able to keep it up for two mornings because his wife needed extra help getting their children ready for school. The third week he did not make it at all because he had stayed up late several nights watching the season finales of his favorite shows and couldn't get up in the morning to do the writing and make it to work on time. By the fourth week he gave up.

A few months later he asked me to help him achieve his goal of writing the book. I said yes, but only if he was committed to the Infinichi Coaching process. He took the Five Element Quiz and discovered that he was the Fire Element/Passionate Personality type. I advised him to start on the Five Element + Fire Element herbal supplement program to optimize his core element and to balance it with the other elements. I explained to him that the Fire/Passionate person gets excited about an idea or project but the "fire" tended to fizzle out when he or she encountered blockages. I taught him a body-mind chi gong practice to reinforce his Fire Element energy.

In order to leverage his Fire Element strengths I told him he needed to be "inspired" regularly to keep his passion fire going. I suggested that he try changing the writing venue based on the setting or the plot of his novel. We brainstormed several locations, including local coffee houses, libraries, museums, a beach parking lot with a stunning view of the ocean, and an ornately designed landmark building where the main character in his story worked. I also talked to him about being realistic with scheduling and to work with his wife so that he gets every other Saturday afternoon "off" for 3–4 hours so that he can do his writing at these various places. Naturally he was enthusiastic and off he went.

Every other week we met for half an hour either in person or via online video conferencing. During some sessions, we tried to troubleshoot his writer's block, which I determined to be due to some faulty mechanics in dialogue. So I suggested that he get out of his mind and talk to real people of various ages and backgrounds to validate or improve on the dialogue of his characters. The Fire Personality gets inspiration from interactions with others. At the end of each session we would agree on assignments to be completed by the next coaching session and at the beginning of each session I held him accountable for his actions. By the end of the seventh month of our coaching work together, he finally completed the draft of the book, well ahead of the deadline he had set originally. The Infinichi Coaching process relies on Five Element Personality knowledge to decipher the blockages that prevent forward movement in one's life and to advice on practices and techniques to clear the obstacles so the person can get back on track.

Appendix

Wood Element Chi Gong
(Instructional videos available through Infinichi.com.)

Wood Element Chi Gong is specifically designed to help detoxify the liver and symptoms associated with a wood imbalance and to clear the liver.

Start by standing with your feet shoulder width apart and curl your tongue so the bottom tip is touching the roof of your mouth.

Inhale, step forward diagonally with your right leg and exhale.

Inhale, and bring your arms up on the sides above your head.

Exhale, and bring your hands down in the middle with your hand facing downward, slowly moving them over your liver and use the motion of pushing down the right leg. Repeat several times, pushing down your legs and out of your toes with your big toe pushing upward to activate the Liver Channel. Visualize blockages and toxins in your liver being brought down your leg and pushed out the big toe.

Return your feet to shoulder width apart and take a deep breath and relax your body.

Inhale and bring your arms up on the side of your body, stopping above your head. Exhale and bring your hands down the center. Circle your hands around your back at your abdomen and return them to the center facing down and then back to your sides.

Standing with your feet shoulder width apart, inhale and begin by circling your hands upward and out to the sides until you reach shoulder level into the middle with your hands facing upward. Bring your hand up and with a pushing motion downward in front of your body.

Inhale, and bring your arms upward and gently rest your middle finger tips on your shoulder at the Jian Jing or Mid-Shoulder point.

Inhale, and visualize bringing your breath from your abdomen to your perineum, up your spine and exhale down your arms through your middle fingers and down your trunk and through your legs out the bottom of your feet.

Repeat this several times and circle your hands around your back at your abdomen and return them to the center facing down and then back to your sides between each practice.

Slowly raise your hands above your head in the center and with a pushing motion, bring them back down to your sides.

Fire Element Chi Gong

(Instructional videos available through Infinichi.com.)

Fire Element Chi Gong is designed to help calm anxiety, reduce stress, promote healthy circulation, and relieve symptoms related to heart health.

Begin with an inhale, and from the sides of your body, gently raise your arms to your head with your palms facing up. When you reach your head, turn your palms so that they face the top of the head at the acupoint Hundred Meeting (DU-20).

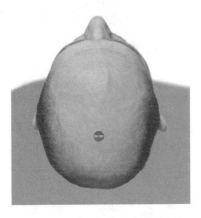

Exhale, imagining that you are exhaling through the centers of your palm (at the Labor Palace acupoint) into the top of your head.

Inhale, and then exhale, gently bringing your arms

down with your palms facing down. At about head level, start exhaling out of the middle of your palms. Visualize bringing the energy down through your lower abdomen. End by turning your palms so that they face your abdomen.

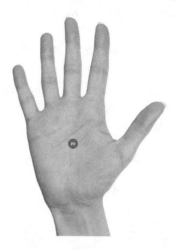

At this point, your arms should be curved and relaxed at about waist level. Hold this posture, gently breathe, and meditate.

Inhale, and bring the energy up from the perineum to the top of your upper back just below cervical vertebrae (the vertebrae in your neck).

Exhale, imagining you are exhaling down the inside of your left arm, out of the Labor Palace point, and into your lower abdomen.

Inhale from the middle of your palms and bring then energy up your left arm, to the center of your chest. Exhale, and visualize the energy moving down and around your lower abdomen, starting down your right side and finishing up around your left side.

Inhale, and bring the energy up from your perineum to the top of your upper back just below the cervical vertebrae.

Exhale down your right arm, out of the middle of your palms and into the lower abdomen.

Inhale from the middle of your palms and bring the energy up your right arm to the center of your chest.

Exhale, and visualize the energy moving down and around your lower abdomen, starting down your left side and finishing up around your right side.

Inhale from the center of your left sole, bringing the energy up your left leg, to your thigh, and then your hip.

Exhale, and visualize the energy moving around your abdomen, starting up your lower left side, to the top of the abdomen, down your right side and ending up around the left side of your lower abdomen.

Inhale from the center of your right sole, bringing the energy up your right leg, to your thigh, and up to your hip.

Exhale, and visualize the energy moving around your lower abdomen, starting from your right side, to the top, down your left side, and ending up at the right side of your lower abdomen.

Inhale, and visualize the energy at the top of the head moving down to the center of your chest.

Exhale, and visualize the energy moving around your lower abdomen, starting up the top, moving down your left side, and ending up at the right side of your lower abdomen.

Begin to return the chi to your body.

Inhale, bringing your hands to your sides. Then with your palms facing toward your back, gather the energy around you (making a circle), bringing your arms in front of you, with your palms facing your lower abdomen.

Exhale, visualizing the gathering energy entering your lower abdomen and swirling around the navel.

Quickly inhale, and slowly raise your hands with your palms facing down and level with your lower abdomen.

Exhale, and bring the energy back to your lower abdomen.

Repeat this exercise twice a day. In evening, do this exercise before 7 p.m.

Earth Element Chi Gong

(Instructional videos available through Infinichi.com.)

Earth Energy Chi Gong is designed to help strengthen the stomach and entire digestive track to assist with symptoms of fatigue, bloating and other digestive functions. Most of this exercise is visualization of energy disks in your abdomen.

Begin with your feet shoulder-width apart and bring your arms up on the sides and pausing in the middle with your hands facing downward over your head. Inhale, and visualize bringing your breath from your abdomen to your perineum, up your spine and out of your palms toward the top of your head.

Bring your arms and hands downward with your palms facing toward your abdomen, similar to if you were holding a ball against your stomach. Hold your arms there for the visualization.

Inhale, and visualize rotating a disk parallel to your body in your abdomen, centered at your navel, in a full rotation first clockwise and then counter-clockwise. Repeat three times with each rotation.

Next visualize the disk being horizontal to your abdomen, centered at your navel, with half of the disk outside your body and half inside. Breath slowly, deeply and with intent while holding the posture.

Inhale and visualize the disk rotating a full rotation first clockwise and then counter-clockwise. Repeat three times with each rotation.

Next visualize the disk being vertical to your abdomen, centered at your navel, with half of the disk outside your body and half inside dividing left and right. Inhale and visualize the disk rotating a full rotation first clockwise and then counter-clockwise. Repeat three times with each rotation.

Inhale and bring your arms up on the side. Exhale and bring your hands down the center. Circle your hands around your back at your abdomen and return them to the center facing down and then back to your sides.

Metal Element Chi Gong
(Instructional videos available through Infinichi.com.)

Metal Element Chi Gong is specifically tailored to help strengthen your body, support the vital organs, healthy immunity, and balance the hormonal functions.

Begin in a standing position with your feet shoulder-width apart. Bend down at the waist and touch the floor with your palms stretched shoulder-width apart. Bend your knees slightly. This should create an upside-down V – your buttocks should be pointing up while your feet and palms are firmly planted on the floor. Similar to the yoga stance of Downward Dog.

Inhale gently and deeply while focusing your attention on your perineum, the area between the genitals and anus. Imagine the inhalation is drawing air in through the perineum.

As you exhale, start to bend your knees as you begin to transfer your weight backward onto your legs. In a sweeping downward and forward motion, bring your chest close to the floor, ending in a modified push-up posture. Your legs should be straight and slightly above the floor, your back arched up starting from the waist, your hands pushing against the floor directly below your shoulders, your arms straight, and your eyes looking forward (not down or up). As you exhale, focus your attention on the center of your palms, imagining the exhalation going out through the palms into the ground.

As you inhale again, focus on the perineum and return to the starting upside-down V position.

Repeat the exhale-inhale steps above 5 times, and work your way up to 10 times or more.

Water Element Chi Gong

(Instructional videos available through Infinichi.com.)

Water Element Chi Gong is designed to help your Kidney and Bladder Channel which can become out of balance and lead to kidney and bladder infections, reproductive issues, lower back pain, and premature aging.

To begin, stand with your feet shoulder width apart, legs slightly bent and arms draped at your sides. Bring your hands around to your lower back at the kidneys and pull the energy from the back, bending and touching your knees with your hands, moving the energy to your knees and out your feet. Repeat several times.

Return to standing with your feet shoulder width apart, legs slightly bent and arms draped at your sides. Bring your arms up in front of you to the level of our forehead, hands not touching and facing your forehead. Staying in this position, visualize connecting the energy from your abdomen, to the perineum and up the spine and down your arms and out your palms.

Move your hands above your head to the Hundred Meeting Point. Again, visualize moving the energy again from your abdomen, to the perineum, up the spine, down your arms and out of your palms to the Hundred Meeting Point.

Move your hands down to your abdomen (as if you are holding a ball in front of your navel) and visualize circulating the energy again in a continuous loop. From your abdomen, to the perineum, up the spine, down the arms and out your palms to your abdomen. Keep moving the energy in this circular motion several times.

Finish by circling your hands around your back at your abdomen and return them to the center facing down and then back to your sides between each practice.

Foundation Practice

As a foundation practice, this practice can be done alone or as a warm-up before your elemental exercise. By tapping the trunk, arms, and legs, you activate the flow of energy and blood in your body. Practice the warm-up for 15 minutes – or more – every day.

Stand with your feet shoulder-width apart, spine erect, and head tilted slightly forward.

Make your right hand into a loose fist and begin tapping your lower abdomen with mild to moderate strength in a rhythmic fashion. Proceed to the middle and upper abdomen, then the chest.

Start tapping under the armpit of the left arm, then the inner part of the arm and down to the palm. Then tap the outer part of the arm back up to the shoulder. Tap the shoulder muscle 7 times.

Repeat the same movement with the left hand.

Begin tapping the lower back on both sides with both hands in loose fists. Move the tapping down the back of the legs to the outsides of the ankles.

Start tapping on the insides of the ankles, working your way up the insides of the calves and thighs.

Finally, return to a standing position, again tapping your lower abdomen. End by placing your palms on your lower abdomen, left hand on the top of the right. Make clockwise circles, rubbing the lower abdomen 36 times.

Lose Weight and Keep Your BMI (Body Mass Index) Below 25

How to Calculate Your BMI:
Formula: weight (lb) / [height (in)]2 x 703
Calculate BMI by dividing weight in pounds (lbs) by height in inches (in) squared and multiplying by a conversion factor of 703.

Example: Weight = 150 lbs, Height = 5'5" (65")
Calculation: [150 ÷ (65)2] x 703 = 24.96

What Your BMI Calculation Means:
Weight Status
Below 18.5 Underweight
18.5 – 24.9 Normal or Healthy Weight
25.0 – 29.9 Overweight
30.0 and Above Obese

Practice Meditation for Stress Release Daily

Chi Meditation for Stress Release
Pathway Number 1

Inhale, bring your mind to both sides of your head, and exhale, say the word Calm in your mind and feel the sides of your head relax and loosen up. Now inhale, we move your focus and energy down to both sides of your neck, and exhale, say the world Calm as you exhale and feel the neck loosen up and relax. Now inhale, as we move to both shoulders and exhale, Calm, feeling the shoulders lighten and relax. Inhale, now as we move to the upper arms and exhale, Calm, feel the upper arms and all the muscles relax and holding no tension. Inhale, now we move down to your elbows and exhale, Calm, you are completely relaxed and feel the muscle in that area relax. Inhale, then to both forearms and exhale, Calm, feel the forearms relax. Inhale, now we move to the wrists, and exhale, Calm, the wrists now are free of tension. Inhale and now we move to the back of both hands and exhale, Calm, feel the back of your hands relax. Inhale, now all your upper torso and arms should be feeling tension free and relaxed with the energy flowing to all 10 fingers and converge at the tip of both middle fingers for about one minute. So focus your mind, your attention and your breath at the tip of your middle fingers. Breathe slowly, deeply and smoothly and each time you exhale say the word calm silently in your mind and continue to focus at the tip of both middle fingers. (Silent focus for 1 minute)

If you need to get going with the rest of your day, it is now time to return your energy to the source. Slowly come out of your deep relaxation, try and gather and concentrate your energy back to your dantian or energy center in your lower abdomen. We need to gather the energy back to the storehouse and as you move and visualize the energy flowing back into that area beneath your belly button, place your left palm against your abdomen and the right hand covers the left hand.

Move your hands starting from small circles and gradually increasing to larger and larger circles in a clockwise direction for 36 times and then repeat this in the opposite direction also 36 circles counterclockwise. When you have finished your routine and you need to wake up simply rub both hands together to generate heat and cup the palms over your eyes to warm them and repeat this three times followed by massaging your eyes, your nose and ears.

For More Pathways and the complete meditation visit taostar.com.

Merry-Go-Round Exercise

Merry-Go-Round is a simple walking exercise that can easily be done for anyone, including those with health conditions that exclude them from vigorous exercises.

In a quiet outdoor setting – a park or yard – find a tree with at least five feet of clear space around the trunk in all directions. If you were to draw a circle around the tree, its diameter would be around 10 to 12 feet, though larger or smaller circles are also fine. Perform the following walking exercise for 15 minutes twice a day.

First, walk clockwise around the tree, and with each completed circle, change the position of your arms by slightly raising or lowering your hands in front or at the sides of your trunk.

Halfway though, reverse the circles, walking counterclockwise around the tree, and again, with each completed circle, change the position of your arms by slightly raising or lowering your hands in front or at the side of your trunk.

Acupoint Liver 3

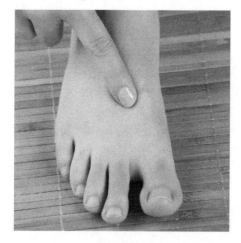

Acupoint Heart 7

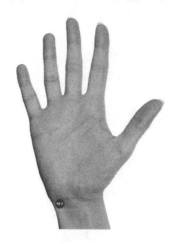

Acupoint Spleen 3

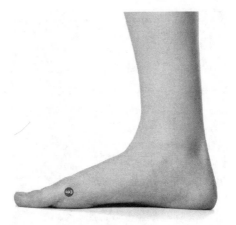

Acupoint Lung 9

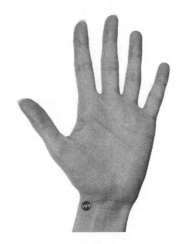

Acupoint Kidney 3

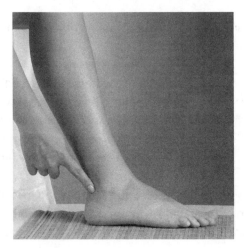

Know My Gifts

Here I am happy to share my own answers to the questions.

Question: What is my Element/Personality Type?
Answer: I am Water Element/Wise Personality. My strength is in big picture vision, strategic planning, and facilitating exchange of constructive knowledge and information. I love learning, teaching and coaching.

Question: What is my life purpose beyond myself?
Answer: To be an instrument for positive change and transformation in people's health and lives.

Question: If I didn't have to work to make a living, what would I be doing and how will those dreams help me fulfill my life purpose?
Answer: I would be helping people improve their health (as a doctor), empowering people with knowledge and tools for changing themselves and their lives (as an author and coach), and providing opportunities for positive life transformations (infinichi. com).

Question: How can I use my abilities and talents to serve others and who will benefit from my dreams?
Answer: My work will serve everyone who is interested in better health, relationships, financial

conditions and happiness. Our clinics (Tao of Wellness), schools of Chinese medicine (Yo San University), meditation and Tai Chi studies (College of Tao), wellness products and financial opportunities (Infinichi), are all ways I plan to make a difference in people's lives.

Question: When I fast forward my dream to the end and look back, what do I wish to see?
Answer: I wish to see many people's health improved by the healing services that my team of doctors and I have provided. I wish to see people having discovered themselves, become empowered and actualized their potential and dreams in their own lives. Finally, I wish to see the world in a more peaceful, healthier and happier place.

Here Are Mine, What's Yours?

Here I share my own answers to the questions:

Question: Why am I here? What is my life purpose?
Answer: 1) I am here to actualize my full unique potential, and 2) to be an instrument for positive change and transformation in people's health and lives.

Question: If today I didn't have to work to make a living, what would I be passionately doing?
Answer: I would be passionately helping people to restore their health, experience peace and improve their lives.

Question: When I fast forward my life to the end and reflect back on my entire life, what do I wish to see?
Answer: I wish to see my family living happily, people's health and lives impacted positively by my efforts, have traveled to many countries and learned about different cultures, made good friends on every continent and lived in harmony with the Divine.

Index

A

Actualized Life 282
Acupoint Liver 165
Acupoint Spleen 172, 342
Acu-Release Technique 164

C

Chi gong 35, 38, 52, 69, 103, 157, 226, 322
Codonopsis root 74
Commitment 293
Correct financial attitude 212

E

Earth Element 7, 17, 59, 60, 62, 63, 67, 68, 69, 70, 71, 74, 134, 135, 138, 170, 171, 172, 196, 197, 198, 199, 213, 226, 229, 248, 278, 287, 288, 301
7, 17, 59, 60, 62, 63, 67, 68, 69, 70, 71, 74, 134, 135, 138, 170, 171, 172, 196, 197, 198, 199, 213, 226, 229, 248, 278, 287, 288, 301
ART 172
Balance 72

Body 73
Career Possibilities 248, 249
Chi Gong 339
Color 71
Compatibility 197
Diet 135, 137, 138
Digestive Solutions 135
Energy 68, 74, 134, 136, 138
Faithfulness 196
Financial Advice 229
Harmonizing Meditation 199
Health 170
Herb 74
Invocation 171
Love 198
Metabolic Solutions 137
Personality 60, 61, 62, 64, 70
Season 63, 67
Solutions 170
Tips 287
Emotional problems 158
Erectile dysfunction 150

F

Financial corruption 216
Enslavement by Money 218
Greed 217

Miser 216
Financial Energy Transforma-
   tion 219
Financial Inventory 224
Fire Element
   7, 17, 41, 46, 48, 49, 56,
   128, 129, 130, 132,
   166, 167, 168, 186,
   191, 192, 193, 194,
   195, 199, 203, 207,
   226, 228, 247, 278,
   286, 287, 322, 329
   ART 168
   Body 46
   Calming Solutions 131
   Career Possibilities 247
   Chi Gong 329
   Color 49
   Compatibilities 193
   Diet 132, 133
   Energizing Solutions 129
   Energy 42, 43, 47, 50, 55,
      56, 128, 129, 130, 166,
      191, 194, 195, 199,
      203, 207
   Financial Advice 228
   Harmonizing Meditation
      195
   Health 166
   Herb 56
   Invocation 167
   Love 194
   Personality 44, 45, 53,
      54, 213
   Season 63

Solutions 166
Tips 286
Five Element Personality
   Type 12
Five Healths 114

G

Goals 268, 269, 270, 271
   Bite-Sized 271
Golden thread 313

I

I Ching 11, 12, 16, 17, 19,
   157, 303
Wood Element 7, 17, 21,
   22, 23, 25, 26, 27, 29,
   30, 34, 35, 37, 39, 114,
   115, 120, 121, 122,
   124, 126, 162, 163,
   165, 188, 189, 190,
   191, 201, 226, 227,
   246, 278, 283, 285, 325
   Appropriateness 188
   ART 165
   Body 35, 124
   Calming Solutions 123
   Career Possibilities 246
   Chi Gong 325
   Compatibilities 189
   Detox Solutions 121
   Diet 126, 127
   Energy 24, 25, 29, 30, 34,
      38, 126, 246
   Financial Advice 227

Flower 39
Harmonizing Meditation 191
Health 162
Health Solutions 162
Invocation 163
Love 190
Path to moral health 188
Personality 22, 28, 186, 242
Primary Color 34
Restoring Solutions 125
Season 23
Stress 122
Time of day 36
Tips 285
Infertility 150
Infinichi Coaching 7, 164, 255, 256, 281, 304, 321, 322, 323

K

Kidney-adrenal energy 146
kidney-adrenal energy network 150

L

Liver energy 30, 32, 120, 122, 123, 162

M

Menstrual irregularity 150
Mentor 303

Metal Element 7, 17, 18, 77, 78, 79, 80, 81, 82, 83, 85, 86, 92, 140, 141, 144, 174, 175, 176, 200, 201, 202, 203, 226, 230, 249, 273, 276, 278, 288, 289, 337
ART 176
Balance 83, 87
Body 86
Career Possibilities 249
Chi Gong 337
Color 85
Compatibility 201
Diet 144, 145
Energy 86, 92, 140, 141, 142, 144, 174
Enhancement Solutions 141
Financial Advice 230
Harmonizing Meditation 203
Health 174
Herb 92
Invocation 175
Love 202
Personality 78, 79, 84, 89
Protective Solutions 143
Season 81
Solutions 174
Tips 288
Mind health 156
Monetary Energy Corruption 215

N

No mind 108

S

Self-awareness 160
Self-care 119, 186
Source of financial energy
    222, 223
Southern, Margaret 221
Sridharan, Anu 310
Start-up 240
    five fundamentals 240
    Adjust and Refuel 243
    Exit or Keep On Going 244
    Know Your Gifts 240
    Make a Road Map 241
    Roll Out and Shout Out
        242

T

Tai chi 32, 35, 38, 52, 69, 103,
    137, 157
Tao 4, 16, 345

V

Valuation tool 214
Vision 25, 34, 39, 101, 204,
    244, 250, 254, 255,
    268, 286, 312, 344

W

Water Element

7, 18, 95, 96, 98, 99, 100,
    101, 102, 105, 110,
    146, 147, 148, 149,
    150, 151, 152, 153,
    178, 179, 180, 204,
    205, 206, 207, 226,
    231, 237, 250, 278,
    285, 289, 344
ART 180
Balance 99
Body 100
Career Possibilities 250
Color 102
Compatibilities 205
Diet 147, 151, 152, 153
Energy 100, 103, 104,
    109, 110, 146, 148,
    150, 151, 178
Financial Advice 231
Harmonizing Meditation
    207
Health 178
Herb 110
Invocation 179
Love 206, 207
Personality 97
Rejuvenation Solutions
    151
Relaxing Solutions 149
Season 98
Solutions 178
Stress 148
Tips 289

RESOURCES

Tao of Wellness Health Center

Santa Monica, CA
310-917-2200
www.taoofwellness.com

Pasadena, CA
626-397-1000
www.taoofwellness.com

Newport Beach, CA
949-706-7770
www.taoofwellness.com

The Tao of Wellness Health Center is the integral way to total wellbeing and a long life. Each patient is seen as an individual whose health is immediately affected by his or her lifestyle including diet, habits, emotions, attitude, and environment. The center, co-founded by Drs. Daoshing and Mao Shing Ni, focuses on acupuncture and Chinese herbs for complete health, longevity, and fertility.

Infinichi
800-772-0222; 310-260-0013
www.infinichi.com
customerservice@infinichi.com

Nourishing Chinese herbal products from the 38th-generation Ni Family Healing tradition. Books on your individual element to nurture the spirit and to provide tools for positive living. Tai Chi and chi gong on DVD, and guided meditation on CD. Infinichi provides the products you need to create a happier, healthier life!

Yo San University
Traditional Chinese Medicine & Clinic
Los Angeles, CA
877-967-2648; 310-577-3000
www.yosan.edu
admissions@yosan.edu

One of the finest and most academically rigorous Traditional Chinese Medicine schools in the United States, Yo San University offers a fully accredited Master's and Doctoral degree programs in acupuncture, herbology, tuina body work, and chi movement arts. In this program, students explore their spiritual growth as an integral part of learning the healing arts.

Chi Health Institute

Los Angeles, CA
www.collegeoftao.com
contact@collegeoftao.com

The Chi Health Institute (CHI) offers professional education and certification in the Ni family chi movement arts including tai chi, chi gong, and Taoist meditation.

College of Tao

Los Angeles, CA
www.collegeoftao.com
contact@collegeoftao.com

Learn about classical Taoist teachings transmitted by the Ni family through books, mentoring, and retreats organized by the College of Tao. The COT assists people in achieving physical, mental, and spiritual health by nurturing self-respect and by offering methods of self-improvement based on the principles in the classic works of the I Ching and Lao Tzu's Tao Teh Ching.

Chinese Nutrition: Distance Learning Course
www.taostar.com

Apply the classic concepts and power of Traditional Chinese Medicine to the selection of daily foods. Basic understanding and practical application of nutrition theories including food energetics, survey of Zang-Fu syndromes, and patient consultation. Up to 45 hours of CEU credit available for licensed acupuncturists.

Infinichi Institute International
PO Box 26712
San Jose, CA 95159-6712
408-295-5911
www.longevity-center.com

Professional training in chi healing leading to certification as an InfiniChi Practitioner. The program is designed to develop your energetic healing abilities utilizing the Ni family books and texts that relate to Traditional Chinese Medicine, chi gong, Chinese bodywork, and natural spirituality. It features a progressive, systematic program that nurtures understanding, facilitates skill development, and promotes self-growth.

Other Titles

Chi Gong for Your Element:
Promote Health and Well-Being, Create Balance in Your Element

Price: $19.95

Chi Gong for your Element Type combines the need for mental clarity and physical health in one gentle self-healing movement. Specifically tailored for each element's own individual strengths and weaknesses to optimize your health, achieve relaxation and return your body to its natural shape. This practice is broken down into two easy to follow sections for both beginners and experts can enjoy following along with Dr. Mao.

Energy Harmonizing Meditations for Your Element
Guided By: Dr. Mao Shing Ni

Price: $12.95

Welcome to your path to serenity, healing and happiness. In Energy Harmonizing Meditation, Dr. Mao Shing Ni will lead you on an inspiring audio meditation drawn from his family's ancient healing practices to help you unlock the highest potential of your individual element. Dr. Mao will share the essential tenants of Chinese Medicine, including the principles of self-healing, the nature of chi, a description of the Elemental personality types and much more! With our guided meditation you will have a set of tools to maintain a healthy state of mind that leads to a deeper sense of peace and happiness.

Secrets of the I Ching: Your Personality

Price: $9.95

Every person is a combination of all five elements, Wood, Fire, Earth, Metal and Water, but you have only one core element that unlocks your personality. Once you understand what your element is, you can begin connecting to a more complete picture of yourself.

This booklet offers you an introduction to the unique attributes of your individual personality. Through this guide you will begin to transform imbalances and tune into the powers and unique gifts that rejuvenate your higher purpose. Topics include career, financial, relationships, fung shui, mental, nutrition, and much more!

Both practical and insightful, Infinichi's Element Booklet offers you inspiring wisdom to achieve your journey towards happiness and fulfillment!

Five Elements: The Balance and Longevity Formula
– 240 capsules

A powerful whole body tune-up, combining pure concentrated extracts of all the herbs that support the Wood, Fire, Earth, Metal and Water elements. A natural, whole food combination of 42 traditional Chinese herbs to support healthy function of the five bodily systems to promote physical vitality, high tolerance for stress, strong immunity, a clear mind, suppleness of body, healthy digestion, normal appetite, proper fluid metabolism and balanced hormonal function.

Wood ELEMENT: Herbal Support for an Authoritative, Positive Spirit
Liver Energy Network
Detox and Nervous System Function

The Wood formula promotes the ability of the liver to cleanse our bodies of environmental pollutants from our air, water and food; and clear the internal toxins that are created by our reaction to anxiety and stress. The smooth flow of Liver Chi energy balances our nervous system, gives us mental clarity and focus, and supports our ability to be powerful problem solvers. Signs of Wood imbalance: Irritability, impatience, extremism, anxiety, problems with vision, muscle tension or spasm, indigestion, insomnia, disturbed dreams, confusion.

FIRE ELEMENT: Herbal Support for a Passionate, Joyful Spirit
Heart Energy Network
Brain and circulatory function

The Fire element is extraordinary because it acts as a connection between the body and the mind. When the energy within this system is abundant, the brain is nourished, the mind is clear and focused, the senses are keen, the memory is sharp, the heart is robust and the cardiovascular system is open. The Shen, or spirit, is joyful.

Signs of Fire imbalance: Heart or blood pressure problems, palpitations, anxiety, excess worry, emotional sensitivity, anxiety, insomnia, poor memory or lack of focus.

Earth ELEMENT: Herbal Support for a Caring, Stable Spirit
Stomach Energy Network
Digestion and metabolism function

The Earth element corresponds to the digestive system. A balanced Earth person looks and feels robustly healthy. The Earth formula supports and stimulates healthy digestion, which in turn improves the absorptions of nutrients.

Vibrant, well-nourished stomach energy encourages normal metabolism and gives us the ability prevent problems before they become a serious threat.

Sign of Earth imbalance: Stomach or digestion problems, bloating, weight issues, food cravings, blood-sugar swings, lack of energy, excessive worry and meddling.

Metal ELEMENT: Herbal Support for a Strong, Determined Spirit
Lung Energy Network
Immunity and lung function

The Metal element acts like a shield to protect us from the external invasion of illness. In classic Chinese theory, the Metal element promotes strong immune function and robust recovery from disease. The theory also notes that the organ most prone to invasion by colds and flu is the lung; because prevention is key, maintaining healthy lung energy is a good place to start.

Signs of Metal imbalance: vulnerability to illness, respiratory and skin conditions, inflexibility, negativity or sadness, climate or temperature sensitivity, difficulty with change.

Water ELEMENT: Herbal Support for a Wise, Determined Spirit
Kidney Energy Network
Adrenal and hormone Function

The Water element formula enhances our Jing, the root force of life; it is also responsible for hormone system reserve, water metabolism, physical stamina and reproductive health. In Traditional Chinese Medicine, vigorous Kidney energy maintains the delicate balance of hormones for normal growth, maturation and robust aging of the human organism.

Signs of Water imbalance: low tolerance for stress, hormone imbalance, kidney, urinary or adrenal problems, emotional inaccessibility, hair loss and fertility or libido challenges.

Ancient Treasures Tea

Ancient Treasures is a delightful combination of three notable traditional Chinese tea collections: cleansing herbs to smooth and strengthen the flow of CHI our life force energy; circulation-enhancing herbs to nourish our JING, our life force essence; and relaxing herbs to calm and soothe the SHEN, our spirit...our soul. An all vegan, caffeine and naturally gluten free exclusive product from Infinichi.

Cleansing/Detox: Beautiful yellow chrysanthemum flowers are well known for their ability to detox and calm the liver, which with the addition of fragrant Chinese mint, allows constrained liver energy to run freely.

Circulation Enhancing: History tells us that there is no better herb for strengthening and gladdening the heart than Chinese motherwort, while white mulberry leaves and wooly grass roots are used in traditional Chinese medicine to calm and cool agitated blood.

Calming/Relaxing: Lily bulb, of stunning lotus blossom fame, and chamomile flowers contain anti-anxiety properties that have been used for treating stress and insomnia for thousands of years, while licorice root is a classic for harmonizing all the herbs in this spirit-soothing formula.

A Trio of Exclusive Formulations, Crafted with Nature's Finest Ingredients for Gentle Skincare and Protection

Renewing Cleanser

One dab of richly-lathering Chinese botanicals, Vitamin C and beta carotene purifies, protects and energizes while chamomile, coconut and alba bark lock in vital moisture.

Radiant Day Cream

Proprietary Chinese herbals plus luminescent pearl powder, zinc oxide, grape stem cells and hotosomes provide natural daytime defense and deliver nourishing hydration in a sumptuous, shine-free formula.

Regenerating Night Cream

A silky emollient fortified with Chinese herbs and luxurious pearl powder along with healing botanicals and antioxidants in an easily absorbed, velvety soy, sesame and avocado base.